T0195695

RETROFIT

Becoming complete
through spiritual growth

Charlie Hatchett

WESTBOW
PRESS®
A DIVISION OF THOMAS NELSON
& ZONDERVAN

This book is a work of non-fiction. Unless otherwise noted, the author and the publisher make no explicit guarantees as to the accuracy of the information contained in this book and in some cases, names of people and places have been altered to protect their privacy.

WestBow Press books may be ordered through booksellers or by contacting:

WestBow Press
A Division of Thomas Nelson & Zondervan
1663 Liberty Drive
Bloomington, IN 47403
www.westbowpress.com
844-714-3454

Because of the dynamic nature of the Internet, any web addresses or links contained in this book may have changed since publication and may no longer be valid. The views expressed in this work are solely those of the author and do not necessarily reflect the views of the publisher, and the publisher hereby disclaims any responsibility for them.

Any people depicted in stock imagery provided by Getty Images are models, and such images are being used for illustrative purposes only. Certain stock imagery © Getty Images.

Scripture quotations taken from the (NASB®) New American Standard Bible®, Copyright © 1960, 1971, 1977, 1995, 2020 by The Lockman Foundation. Used by permission. All rights reserved. www.lockman.org

Scripture quotations taken from The Holy Bible, New International Version® NIV® Copyright © 1973 1978 1984 2011 by Biblica, Inc. TM. Used by permission. All rights reserved worldwide.

ISBN: 978-1-6642-7924-7 (sc)
ISBN: 978-1-6642-7923-0 (hc)
ISBN: 978-1-6642-7925-4 (e)

Library of Congress Control Number: 2022917869

Print information available on the last page.

WestBow Press rev. date: 11/10/2022

CONTENTS

INTRODUCTION

How exactly would you react if I tell you that the world of athletics is merely an illusion? I can only imagine what is going through your mind having read the question above.

Before understanding this statement, do not give in to speculation and assumption, or contemplate putting the book back on the shelf or getting your money back. Instead, I encourage you to get through a few chapters of this extraordinary book. Only then will you begin to understand what I am talking about. Also, do not be quick to think I hate or have reservations about sports. On the contrary, just like many Americans, I am an avid lover of sports. In fact, I am a former athlete myself.

As a child, I grew up playing just about everything I could, and I must attest that those were the best times of my life. While I was playing just about any sport I could participate in, it was only then that my mother was able to get some free time to herself after taking me to the various practices and games. It was also a good way of keeping me off the street and preventing me from getting into trouble that could endanger my life. So engaging in sports provided several benefits that I am forever grateful for. Although these benefits are multifaceted in nature, some of them were life changing—they came with a lifetime contract. A contract that many of us have signed without noticing, failing to recognize the length and implications of this contract. It left an indelible imprint on my life and identity that are too obvious to ignore. Before you begin to freak out and start looking frantically for a nonexistent physical contract, there wasn't one. It was an invisible contract that is binding on many athletes till this day.

In 1999, which happened to be my eleventh year of life, I was enjoying every part of my childhood, consumed by ecstasy and free as a bird. Although I didn't have the privilege of a luxurious lifestyle, I had everything I needed and seldom had more than enough. At that time, as an emerging athlete, my sports of choice were basketball and baseball, although basketball took the number one spot in my heart.

I invested all my available time playing basketball—from dawn till dusk. I was that annoying kid who would wake up the neighbors at 6:00 a.m. dribbling the ball on a Saturday morning. No wonder I got several stares and unpleasant gazes from some adult neighbors. Basketball became an integral part of my life. From shopping for candy to playing video games, the ball accompanied me everywhere I went. Some kids went everywhere with their Barbie doll, action figure, blanket, or teddy bear, but for me, my basketball was my Siamese twin. The basketball went with every outfit.

As the summer of 1999 steadily rolled in, my stepdad, who came into my life around the age of 8 years old was a big football fan, asked me for the final time if I wanted to play football. Earlier, I had declined several offers, but to make him happy I decided to give it a try. My first day of Pop Warner was very interesting. Happily, I showed up for football practice with other kids who had played football for at least three years. They curiously looked at me, wondering why I was smiling. Then I was given some pads and within moments, *whack*! I was knocked flat on my back. Some super-experienced twelve year old forcefully hit me so hard during the drill that I slightly blacked out, and this quickly reminded me why I had never tried playing football. After my first practice, my stepdad took me home, correcting me about the errors I committed during the practice. I wore a sad look and loudly blurted, "Dad, I don't want to play football anymore!"

This spurred my stepdad to motivate me. Being a super fan of football, he encouraged me not to quit. Although usually he didn't force me to do anything, he encouraged me to try football for one year. If I didn't like it, I could quit playing forever.

Amazingly, every passing day, my performance considerably improved. Within the first month, I moved from second string to first string, and it wasn't difficult for the coach to discover my newfound motivation. For some people, their motivation can be fully rewarded with toys, ice cream, candy, a job, or commendation, but not me. None of these is potent enough to keep me playing football. Instead, I was told that someone wanted to hurt one of my family members and that I needed to do something about it. What a terrible motivation for a kid! This terrifying motivation got me playing at such a level that nobody believed that 1999 was my first year of playing football. As coaches continued to use this horrifying tactic to get me to play at a very high level, our team continued to dominate all other Pop Warner teams across the state and the region. Eventually, we played in the Pop Warner super bowl.

One of the best moments of my life was the chance I got to go to Disney World for the first time in my life. I probably would not have been able to go if it were not for my stepdad putting me on the football team. We played our hearts out in the super bowl that year, but got crushed by the opposing team. Despite the loss, it was a great football year—from clinching the starting role in my position to playing in the super bowl, the dream of every football player at all levels. This feat marked the beginning of a new relationship for me. I went from loving basketball to loving football.

You may ask, "Isn't that normal?" There is nothing wrong with loving one sport over the other. But what you will read in this book is not about this sport or how it changed my life. It's about other sportsmen whose lives have been changed and who are still dealing with the consequences.

Change happens whether we want it or not; it's inevitable. Some people are creatures of habit. They want to keep doing things the same way, every time, while other people are ecstatic about change. They want to try out new things and live a life of variety.

Managing change has become a cottage industry.

Several authors have written books about change; business consultants have made careers analyzing the topic. It is evident that some things are easy to change: clothing, hairstyles, meals, holidays, sports, cars, etc. However, I have discovered that the most important things are not our physical appearances or the ephemerals of life, but what we think and do.

God gave human beings the free will to think, act, and respond to the world around us. He has also shown us, as believers, how we should think and behave. Apostle Paul succinctly addressed this issue in his epistle to the Romans:

> Therefore, I urge you, brethren, by the mercies of God, to present your bodies a living and holy sacrifice, acceptable to God, which is your spiritual service of worship. And do not be conformed to this world, but be transformed by the renewing of your mind, so that you may prove what the will of God is, that which is good

and acceptable and perfect. (Romans 12:1–2
NASB)

As you begin to renew your mind, you will be able to understand the good, acceptable, and perfect will of God for your life. Understanding God's perfect will is the key element of spiritual maturity. It conforms you to biblical ways of thinking and living. Consequently, you will learn to live like our Lord and Savior, Jesus Christ, with the help of the Holy Spirit. And in doing so, you will become retrofit.

1

THE MANUFACTURING PROCESS

"Congratulations! It's a boy," said the doctor to my fourteen-year-old mother. Isn't it amazing that my beautiful, strong, awesome, inspiring, loving mother had me at the young age of fourteen? I was born into this world healthy. As obvious as this may sound, please know that health is a precious gift of God. You and your household must be grateful for your fingers, toes, limbs, organs, and healthy bodies. I'm always thankful and in awe of God for granting me the grace to start life in good health and vitality.

Many of us grew up with both our parents, but in my case, I was only nurtured by my mother for the first 8 years of my life until my stepfather came into the picture to help in my development. My mother and I did everything together, and as expected, we became inseparable.

THE GOLDEN SEED

All of us are born with what I call a "planted seed" inside us. If I may speak to you like a farmer, that seed is planted in a jiffy but requires nurturing and time to sufficiently grow and blossom. It is incredible to note that when the seed has fully grown, it produces whatever it was intended to produce. It will benefit our world and those around us.

In other words, we are all born with gifts. These gifts are inherent in us, not outside us. Hence, it isn't necessary to do anything extra to have a gift. However, the availability of gifts doesn't guarantee their efficiency. First, the gift must be discovered, nurtured, and developed. After that, the individual will utilize, enjoy, and bless other people with such gifts.

Once the gift reaches the point of utilization and enjoyment, everyone who meets such a gifted person will benefit from these gifts, and a chain reaction of impact and positive influence begins.

This question is often posed to young people: "What do you want to become when you grow up?" Unfortunately, this frequently asked question has become a cliché, and young people can almost smell it coming a mile away. While many young people are undecided, others have fabricated false responses to get off the hook.

MY EXPERIENCE

Someone once asked me what I wanted to become when I grew up. Unbeknownst to him, I was suffering with an identity crisis. So, I cringed, curled up, and struggled with who I was in the early years of my life.

Growing up with a single parent can take a serious toll on anyone, but for me it had indescribable effects. As a boy, it was my dream to grow up to be a dependable, reliable, and responsible man. But I did not grow up with my father around me, who would have trained and mentored me. Thank God for family members who assisted and attempted to fill the vacuum in their many ways, as well as my stepfather.

My mother and grandmother formed a wall of Gibraltar around me. I also had the privilege of having some caring and loving uncles who were like precious roses in my garden—they made life so beautiful. Having these wonderful people around was precious and priceless, but it still wasn't enough. There was an unfilled void and having these beautiful people around me did not prevent me from being confused about my identity, worth, and value.

All along, I had no inkling of the seed that was inside me. I did not understand that there was something planted in me that needed nurturing and watering to grow. So, as I continued to grow in wisdom and get acquainted with life, I discovered that I had many skills. *Yes! That is it*, I said to myself when I discovered a few of the skills I was created to use. Now I know that these skills are the reason why I am on this planet.

I went on with my life, utilizing my skills to get certain things done, and this brought momentary fulfillment. But the expectations I had about myself were stretched when I started meeting highly talented people. I wanted to be like these people. Although many kids want to be like MJ, my idol was also a superstar basketball player, just not the great Michael Jordan. I did all I could to imitate him. I played basketball, had a similar hairstyle, and dressed like him. My strange quest was fueled by previous failures to discover who I was created to be and how to develop my uniqueness. I know several young people are still traveling this difficult path; they desire to be every other person but themselves. I never looked like my favorite basketball player because we are two different people. We just had a shared love for basketball.

Looking back, I can see my errors. I was trying to walk before

I crawled. But disregarding your uniqueness and struggling to become someone you're not is a foolish and dangerous mission.

It is evident that there are voids inside many of us, primarily caused by our failure to discover who we are. Correctly answering this question is the first step to greatness.

I mistakenly thought my skills and talents would answer this question. I ventured into imitating superstars, but this only enlarged the vacuum I was trying to fill. No activity or exercise can fill this void. My numerous attempts were like searching for a needle in a haystack. My eureka moment came when I discovered that there is a divine Creator—the uncreated creator, the almighty God. I realized that I did not create myself; hence, my Creator knows everything about me. This simple revelation became the genesis of my turnaround.

> God created man in His own image, in the
> image of God he created him; male and female
> He created them. (Genesis 1:27 NASB)

Having discovered that I was created in the image of God, the expected next step was to unravel what the image of God looks like. Thankfully, the definition of God's image transcends what we have depicted it to mean. In sending Jesus Christ to the earth to live as a man, God showed us what it truly means to live a life in the image of God. Christ lived an exemplary life of service, goodness, kindness, and love for people regardless of their shortcomings.

In His birth, life, death, resurrection, and ascension, Jesus exemplified the image of God and unveiled its pathway to humankind.

Realizing that I was created in the image of God and understanding how to exude God's image orchestrated my deliverance. Now I no longer pretend to be what I am not nor seek relevance from activities. I had discovered a great truth that would help me along my journey to becoming retrofit.

However, it's important to note that we cannot become retrofit for Christ and His kingdom without first becoming Christlike—this is the first principle of engagement.

TRUE CHANGE BEGINS WITH ATTITUDINAL CHANGE

Attitude is the most pervasive and profound personal characteristic. In fact, changing your attitude is the precursor to changing your mind about anything. Except for salvation, attitudinal change has the greatest single effect on your behavior and success in life.

The Bible is replete with several examples that emphasize the importance of attitudinal change. For instance, in the case of Jacob and Laban, the almighty God intervened by instructing Jacob on what to do, consequently preventing the adverse effects of Laban's attitude.

Laban's sons resorted to blackmailing Jacob, saying, "Jacob has taken everything our father owned and has gained all this wealth from what belonged to our father." Thereafter, it wasn't difficult for Jacob to observe the change in Laban's attitude to him.

> Now Jacob heard the words of Laban's sons, saying, "Jacob has taken away all that was our father's, and from what belonged to our father he has made all this wealth." Jacob saw the attitude of Laban, and behold, it was not friendly toward him as formerly. Then the Lord said to Jacob, "Return to the land of your fathers and to your

relatives, and I will be with you." So, Jacob sent and called Rachel and Leah to his flock and the field, and said to them, "I see your father's attitude, that it is not friendly toward me as formerly, but the God of my father has been with me. You know that I haved served your father with all my strength. Yet your father has cheated me and changed my wages ten times; however, God did not allow him to hurt me. If he spoke thus, 'The speckled shall be your wages,' then all the flock brought forth speckled; and if he spoke thus, 'The striped shall be your wages,' then all the flock brought forth striped. Thus, God has taken away your father's livestock and given them to me. (Genesis 31:1-9 NASB)

At another time, God directly intervened in another situation by changing the heart of a king:

And they observed the Feast of Unleavened Bread seven days with joy, for the Lord had caused them to rejoice, and had turned the heart of the king of Assyria toward them to encourage them in the word of the house of God, the God of Israel. (Ezra 6:22 NASB)

Apostle Paul in his epistle to the Roman believers admonished them about having the right attitude and further elucidated on the changes that occur when this happens.

Now may the God who gives perseverance and encouragement grant you to be of the same mind with one another according to Christ

Jesus, so that with one accord you may with one voice glorify the God and Father of our Lord Jesus Christ. (Romans 15:5-6 NASB)

Apostle Peter revealed the proper attitude toward suffering, which Jesus modeled. It becomes imperative for us as believers to emulate our Lord and Savior, Jesus Christ.

Therefore, since Christ has suffered in the flesh, arm yourselves also with the same purpose, because he who suffered in the flesh has ceased from sin, so as to live the rest of the time in the flesh no longer for the lusts of men, but for the will of God. (1 Peter 4:1–2 NASB)

King Nebuchadnezzar's drastic action toward Daniel's friends was due to a change in his attitude —anger. The passage below highlights how the king's attitude changed and its resultant effect.

Then Nebuchadnezzar was filled with wrath, and his facial expression was altered toward Shadrach, Meshach and Abed-nego. He answered by giving orders to heat the furnace seven times more than it was usually heated. (Daniel 3:19 NASB)

Another definition of attitude is the position of the body to an action or mental state, which is also called posture. For instance, when I am speaking, I can generally read people's responses by the attitude of their bodies or the expressions on their faces.

As human beings, we are creatures of attitude. So do not

underestimate the power of your attitude, because without a good attitude, you can't be retrofitted. I encourage you to ask yourself this question: *Do I have a godly attitude or a worldly attitude? A good attitude about life, or a bad attitude?*

In his book, *The Winning Attitude*, John Maxwell says:

> It is the advance man of our true selves. Its roots are inward, but its fruit is outward. It is our best friend, or our worst enemy. It is more honest and more consistent than our words. It has an outward look based on past experiences. It is the thing which draws people to us or repels them. It is never content until it is expressed. It is the librarian of our past. It is the speaker of our present. It is the prophet of our future. As you look into your history to retrieve past events, your attitude acts as the librarian. You will either be grateful and think about the good things, or you will be ungrateful and think about the bad ones.

Attitude doesn't only archive our past; it is the current speaker in our lives and can accurately prophesy our future. If you have a bad attitude, it will likely keep you from having the future that God or you want to have.

RETROFIT: BE PRICELESS

Ready

> Therefore, if anyone cleanses himself from these things, he will be a vessel for honor, sanctified,

useful to the Master, prepared for every good work. (2 Timothy 2:21 NASB)

Set

Since 1997, MasterCard has received hundreds of awards for their catchy advertisement campaign featuring the slogan "Priceless." As Christians, I think the slogan for our relationships with Christ should be "Serving Is Priceless."

Most people erroneously think that serving is the same as service. I humbly disagree. I believe there is a huge difference between the two. Christ did not come to give good service; He came to serve.

As an athlete, I am not supposed to give good service to my teammates—I am to serve them. As a coach, I serve my team; I do not provide them a service.

Service is something you pay for, or something you expect, such as courteous and prompt attention from the employees at a restaurant or gas station. But serving goes deeper than service. Serving has to do with the heart. It involves making sacrifices and meeting real needs. Christ desires that we as athletes and coaches become servant to our teammates, friends, families, and communities. He desires that we as businesspeople become servants to those who work beside us, above us, or underneath us. He has set us apart for a great work. We are His instruments—His serving instruments! Today, this can be a hard concept to understand. It seems like everyone in the world of sports wants to be a leader, not a servant. Jesus never told us to be leaders, but He instructed us to be servants.

To be a leader you must serve, and this is my challenge to you today. Fulfill Christ's calling on your life and become a servant!

—Dan Britton

Go

1. On a scale of one to five, how well are you serving others (teammates, coaches, friends, family)? Do you give service when Christ demands such from you? If so, when?
2. How has God gifted you to serve? How has He set you apart? Are you serving efficiently?

Workout

Ephesians 2:10; 2 Timothy 2:14–21

Overtime

Lord, teach me how to serve. My teammates, my coworkers, my family, and friends need to see what Jesus looks like through my life. I pray that when I serve, they will be able to see You. Help me to fully understand that You have set me apart for a great work. Amen.

2

THE PREPROGRAMMED MINDSET

Something was still missing after I discovered the new proof of my identity in God. I became ready to begin a new life that was inspiring and exciting. Alas, the previous program in me was still active. Despite coming to a new realization, my mind was not yet changed.

Maybe you were like me and had the opportunity to grow up in a family that was completely loving and accepting of who you are and how you do things. No one condemned you, and you were only held accountable for the things that you were responsible for. What a great way to grow up, right? I wish this were true for most of us. The truth of the matter is, having a caring and loving family doesn't make you immune from being preprogrammed while growing up. If this is your case, know that you are not alone. There are many people who are still struggling with the way they were preprogrammed to this day.

The first couple of months of high school were amazing. I played on the football team, and was not only a starter but one of the top players on the team as a freshman. I played every game of the season the same way I had given unbroken attention to my first love, basketball. Surprisingly, the transition I envisioned ended up being an unpleasant experience no high school freshman would expect. "Pack your things, honey, we are moving to Atlanta," my mom said. At first, I wondered if there was a street in my little town called Atlanta, but I soon found out that she was referring to the city.

I spent the first few months trying to settle in my new nest to having my feathers ruffled up. Atlanta is quite nice, but I needed to adjust to the new life.

My mother exerted all efforts to make me fit in, but it did not work. Eventually, halfway into my freshman year, I convinced my mother to allow me to live with my grandmother so I could attend my hometown high school.

By the time I returned to my former school, the midterm examination was around the corner. The guidance counselor's advice to my grandmother and me was, "He should stay back and repeat his freshman year."

His unsolicited advice had a profound effect on me. I wondered what could have precipitated such a defeating utterance to a young man who was still trying to figure things out after being tossed around from state to state. I felt defeated and humiliated, thinking he could be right. I should have stayed back because it would be difficult to prepare for midterm exams within that short time.

I stood there frozen like a deer in the headlights as dozens of thoughts flooded my overwhelmed mind. Finally, with a stern face, my grandmother turned to me and asked, "Are you stupid"? I sluggishly skewed my head in the direction of my grandma, and replied, "No, Grandma, I am not stupid." Immediately my grandmother told the guidance counselor, "He will not stay back, and he will do everything possible to pass the midterm exam."

The counselor, with a sour look on his face, said OK to my grandmother's statement. He gave us a stack of almost three feet of papers as my homework. Not only did I finish my homework in record time, I also passed the midterm exams with a B average.

That helped my confidence grow tremendously, although I still had a long way to go. Lurking in my heart was doubt and fear; I kept wondering if I would ever pass, accomplish, or complete any tangible thing in life. By this time, my counselor's words had already torn my world apart. I barely believed in myself, and negative thoughts seemed to have overwhelmed me. It is instructive to note that words are mighty—they can build and destroy lives.

Thomas Jefferson once intuitively said: "Nothing can stop the man with a right mental mindset from achieving his goal. Nothing on earth can help the man with the wrong mental mindset." I believe this is true.

Here are some truths to consider as you think about enhancing your attitudes:

1. **You choose your attitudes.**

The Jewish psychiatrist Viktor Frankl was born in Austria in 1905. As an adult, Frankl had the opportunity to get a visa to the United States. He turned it down and chose to stay in Vienna and care for his aging parents. In 1942, Frankl was sent to a Nazi concentration camp. His wife, parents, brother, and sister were also forced into camps.

By the end of the war, only Frankl and his sister had survived. During the three years spent in four different camps, Frankl endured forced labor and witnessed his fellow prisoners dying of starvation and in the gas chamber. Despite all this, Frankl faced suffering with dignity. He chose to forgive and never held a grudge against the Nazi soldiers or the civilians who had given up their Jewish neighbors. Surviving years of unspeakable treatment, Frankl's life became a monument to the human spirit amid suffering.

After regaining freedom in 1945, Frankl returned to Vienna to continue his medical practice and finish his writings about the meaning of life, which he had begun before his arrest. I strongly recommend his book, *Man's Search for Meaning*, which has sold more than twelve million copies in twenty-one languages.

In his book, Frankl described an important philosophy:

> Most important, however, is the third avenue to the meaning in life: even the helpless victim of a hopeless situation, facing a fate he cannot change, may rise above himself, may grow beyond himself, and by so doing change himself. He may turn a personal tragedy into a triumph ... If ... one cannot change his situation, he can still choose his mindset.

Frankl became a lifelong proponent of his now globally accepted form of psychological treatment called logotherapy, which emphasizes the importance of an individual's search for meaning as superior to the search for power or possessions. Frankl continued teaching and writing until his death in 1997 at the age of ninety-two.

2. **Attitudes are not caused by people or circumstances.**

The second truth is derived from the first: people and circumstances do not cause attitudes. We have been deceived to think that a change in circumstances will give us a better mindset. It is not true. Several biblical examples illustrate this truth.

God created Adam and Eve as perfect people. He gave them perfect bodies and placed them in a perfect paradise. God visited, walked, and talked with them in the garden. They had a perfect set of circumstances, but God told them there was only one thing that they could not have—a piece of fruit. Nevertheless, under the serpent's influence, they became ungrateful, rebellious, and disobedient; they took the forbidden fruit and ate it. You could not be in better circumstances than theirs. But they had a bad mindset, which they chose with their own free will.

During the worst season of his life, King David had a fabulous mindset. But during the best time of his life, he exhibited a bad mindset. When King Saul pursued him, people turned against him, and his life was in dire danger, David turned to God in prayer and subsequently wrote psalms. In those difficult seasons, he maintained a godly, humble, and faith-filled mindset. However, when his kingdom became established, David committed adultery with Bathsheba and killed her husband to conceal his misdemeanor. His life illustrates that you cannot solely connect attitudes with people or circumstances.

Apostle Paul went to Philippi to preach the good news about Jesus Christ (Acts 16). The Philippian authorities captured him, beat him with rods, and imprisoned him. But at midnight, Paul wholeheartedly worshipped and praised God. Paul chose his mindset, and it clearly was not connected to his circumstances.

You may be tempted to think, *My mindset is not right, but if my circumstances change, then it would become right.* It simply isn't true.

3. Happiness is a chosen mindset.

Happiness is a chosen mindset rather than just a state of being. Happiness is a state of mind. Many of the greatest comedians emerged from tragic circumstances. Carol Burnett, a brilliant comedian, was the daughter of alcoholic parents and raised by her grandmother. As a child, Carol had neither a bed nor a bedroom; instead, she slept on a couch. She studied under a dim light in the bathroom.

Carol had none of the things that most people would consider requirements for a normal, happy childhood. Despite her circumstances, Carol decided to be happy and to make other people happy.

Some people who have experienced miserable circumstances decide to make life miserable for other people. Others emerge from challenging backgrounds, yet they chose to live and influence other people to live happy lives.

Hugh Downs, a famous journalist and television personality, said, "A happy person is not a person in a certain set of circumstances, but rather a person with a certain set of attitudes." One of my favorite quotes on happiness comes from author Denis Waitley: "Happiness cannot be travelled to, owned, earned, worn, or consumed. Happiness is the spiritual experience of living every minute with love, grace, and gratitude." You may believe that you are headed toward happiness but be sorely disappointed when you arrive at your destination.

You can choose happiness at any point in your life. Through a spiritual transformation, you can begin to live every moment with gratitude to God. It is a mindset, and it is your choice. You can be as miserable as you want to be, or you can be as happy as you choose to be.

4.   **God rewards good attitudes and disciplines bad ones.**
Good parents understand this truth. They don't wait until their
child develops bad behaviors and habits. They discipline while
the problem is still at the mindset level. Of course, God is love,
and like a good parent, He relates to us based on our attitudes.
The Bible speaks about God's disposition to negative attitudes,
He dislikes sinful behaviors such as pride and disobedience.

> But He gives a greater grace. Therefore it says,
> God is opposed to the proud, but gives grace to
> the humble. (James 4:6 NASB)

Pride is a negative mindset, and we can choose to be proud
or humble. The word of God made it clear that God gives grace
to the humble, but He resists the proud. Undoubtedly, God
loves us even when we are full of pride—and we all deal with
pride. However, when we are proud, we are resisting God.
Consequently, God will discipline us. He loves us too much to
ignore us when we are on the wrong path. When we are humble,
we open the door for Him to shower His graces on us, because
He loves and rewards humility. Humility is not the same thing
as humiliation; instead, it is seeing ourselves correctly in God's
light.

> Humble yourselves in the presence of the Lord,
> and He will exalt you. (James 4:10 NASB)

Sometimes all God is waiting for is a change in our attitudes
so that He can bless and give us the things we desire. He loves
us, but He will deal with our negative attitudes. This truth plays
a pivotal role in our spiritual walk and maturity. The author of
the book of Hebrews calls God "Our Father" and emphasizes
how He disciplines us in love.

It is for discipline that you endure; God deals with you as with sons; for what son is there whom his father does not discipline? But if you are without discipline, of which all have become partakers, then you are illegitimate children and not sons. Furthermore, we had earthly fathers to discipline us, and we respected them; shall we not much rather be subject to the Father of spirits, and live? For they disciplined us for a short time as seemed best to them, but He disciplines us for our good, so that we may share His holiness. All discipline for the moment seems not to be joyful, but sorrowful; yet to those who have been trained by it, adfterwards it yields the peaceful fruit or righteousness. Therefore, strengthen the hands that are weak and the knees that are feeble, and make straight paths for your feet, so that the limb which is lame may not be put out of joint, but rather be healed. (Hebrews 12:7–13 NASB)

As your Father, God will discipline you when you err because He loves you, just as any loving human father. Therefore, it becomes imperative for you to love your heavenly Father more than your earthly father. God's plan for you is to give you a glorious life and expected end. Everything He does is for your good—yes, even when He disciplines you. Therefore, it is also essential for you to know that He disciplines in love. This is why the author of Hebrews writes about "the hands which hang down, and the feeble knees."

God deals with you as His amazing child. You know discipline is over when you have learned the lesson. When my wife Virginia and I see that kind of response in our three children, it reminds us that we adults can also misbehave sometimes. God wants us to recognize such negative mindset and its accompanying behaviors.

Therefore, God looks at us and says, "Children, I will deal with your attitudes because I want you to grow and act like me." As a good parent, you discipline your children for their good, so that they will grow up and become responsible adults. God does the same to us because He is by far the best parent.

5. **Attitudes precede and predict your future.**

The fifth truth about attitudes is that they precede and predict your future. You can know many things that will happen in your life because of your attitudes. Good attitudes lead to success, favor, and promotion. Conversely, bad attitudes precede and predict a future of failure, disfavor, and demotion.

Have you heard of the mindset indicator on an airplane? It is a simple instrument that lets you know when you are flying level, climbing, or dropping. The instrument displays a horizontal line, which represents the actual horizon.

A dot above or below the line shows the plane's nose position. Marks on the instrument also indicate the position of the craft's wings, whether they are veering right or left. This vital instrument helps when the pilot cannot see due to clouds or darkness. Any attempt to fly without the mindset indicator, or the inability to interpret it, leaves the plane in danger.

Without it, the pilot only has emotions and personal judgment to guide the plane. Emotions and personal judgment can't determine where the plane is headed, and the results will be disastrous. John F. Kennedy Jr. died because he did not use this instrument correctly. As he was flying at night over the ocean, he lost his visual reference and flew straight into the water.

When you are going through difficulties, don't trust your emotions or people's opinions. God's Word is your mindset indicator. King David, a man of many trials, recorded in the book of Psalms how he focused his eyes on the Lord in the worst times. Through his lifestyle of dependence on God, David showed us the appropriate attitude that we should have when we are going through difficult times. When experiencing a horrible situation and tomorrow looks gloomy, you can turn your eyes to the Word of God. It will help you pick the right mindset rather than being depressed and confused by the noise of your condition.

Abraham Lincoln is considered one of the most remarkable men and one of our greatest presidents. His deep faith in God helped him scale all his hurdles, and it is wise to emulate his life of faith. Many people only know his notable achievements but do not know of the difficult things that Lincoln experienced to become the president of the United States.

Lincoln had a difficult childhood. He had only one year of formal education, and beyond that he taught himself. One of his sisters died in childbirth, and only one of his four sons lived past the age of eighteen. He had a very difficult marriage, had two business failures, and lost six elections. I can imagine the devil coming to him to say, "Lincoln, why don't you just get 'loser' tattooed on your forehead and lay down and die somewhere? What a pathetic loser you are."

Conversely, I can imagine the Holy Spirit whispering these encouraging words to him: "Just keep acting like the president—it's only a matter of time." In the midst of defeat and disappointment, Lincoln never gave up. He allowed God and His Word to sharpen his mindset rather than circumstances. Eventually, Lincoln was elected president of the United States in 1860.

In your life, do not allow circumstances, people, or life's disappointments cause you to have a nose-down mindset. Have you heard the voices as well? You know, those negative, life-debilitating words that Lincoln may have heard to try and deter him from his destiny of being the president of the United States. If you have or are experiencing this, I encourage you to pick your head up and allow your hearing to push past those negative words. Allow your mind to push past those negative thoughts and allow God's Holy Spirit and the encouraging words to fill your ears and mind.

A negative and nose-down mindset will precipitate problems in your life. Stay nose-up and put your faith in God and His Word. Mindset is more necessary than aptitude for success in life. It doesn't matter if other people have better gifts, talent, intellect, or beauty, you can achieve tremendous success provided you have the appropriate mindset.

I once said this quote while speaking to a group of students at Brown University: "In life it is easy to do the hard things, and it is hard to do the easy things." As I was sharing this quote I went on to explain this parable this way. "Suppose you have one person, and they are tasked with having a regular job working 9–5 five days a week, and they are given instruction to take care of themselves through proper eating and exercise. What do you suppose is the tougher of the task? Waking up every morning to commute for one to three hours in traffic to get to work and experience a ton of hardships and rough labor, or taking the time to physically take care of yourself? This individual chose to work and skip out on keeping up with their physical well-being. They worked these hours for months and as time went on their health began to fail. They began to become more tired, unmotivated, and less skillful with their work. They went from worst to worst. In this case they chose the harder things in life.

It is hard to wake up every day and work long hours and dealing with multiple attitudes and personalities. It is easy to take care of your physical well-being, but many will error on the side of the harder and not the easier. Working a career takes a lot of hours in a day but working on yourself takes less than an hour a day. Many have fallen for this trap, which is why it is easy to do the hard things, but hard to do the easy things." And with this attitude, nothing but negativity can become produced in one's life. Negative thoughts, negative emotions, negative habits, and so much more.

6. **Beware the mindset killers.**
Wrong approaches to life and certain negative ways of thinking will destroy your mindset. I call them "mindset killers." Ask yourself if you have ever fallen victim to one of these seven "killers."

False expectations

False (or wrong) expectations can destroy your mindset, especially when you expect every person to treat you well or expect that life will always be easy. Both expectations are a mirage and potential frustrations. In life, you will encounter difficult people and other demanding issues.

"Comparing up"

It is a foolish exercise to compare yourself to other people, especially when they have some advantages that you lack. I call it "comparing up." If you drive into the parking lot and immediately begin to desire all the cars that are nicer than yours, then you are "comparing up." When such thoughts become dominant in your life, they will kill and corrupt your mindset. You must be content with what you have and learn how to count your blessings, not what others possess.

Entitlement mentality

If you begin to think, *Everybody owes me,* you have an entitlement mentality. This mentality is destructive in nature. You must get rid of it because nobody owes you anything.

Negativity

Usually, what do you see, half-filled cups or half-empty cups? Faith in God removes this negativity because faith allows us to view things from the standpoint of positivity.

Pride

Pride is cancerous in nature; it can destroy any glorious destiny. Pride and destruction are Siamese twins; the end of a proud person is predictable.

> Pride goes before destruction, and a haughty spirit before stumbling. (Proverbs 16:18 NASB)

Bitterness

We serve a compassionate God, who is rich in compassion and forgiveness. God expects His children to live like Him. Viktor Frankl could not have continued his remarkable life's work had he nursed bitterness and refused to forgive his enemies.

Self-pity

Self-pity would easily rank as the most dangerous of all mindset killers. When we feel sorry for ourselves, we begin to alter our inner makeup, which leaves no room for the Holy Spirit's power in us. However, marital challenges, financial troubles, and workplace and health issues must not lure you into self-pity.

If you are feeling sorry for yourself because of some circumstances, consider this story: Jerry Long became paralyzed from his neck down his body because of a diving accident in high school. It rendered him a quadriplegic at the age of seventeen. Long learned to use a mouth stick to type and an intercom to communicate. He became a close friend and colleague of Viktor Frankl. Like Frankl, Long did not allow difficult circumstances to dictate his future. In 1990, he earned a doctorate in clinical psychology, and he went on to receive many awards, including the Michael Whiddon Award, the Viktor Frankl International Institute of Logotherapy Medallion of Responsibility, and the Viktor Frankl Award of the City of Vienna. After Victor Frankl passed away in 1997, Long shared the following memory about his friend:

> "Once, after speaking to a large audience, I was asked if I ever felt sad because I could no longer walk. I replied, "Professor Frankl can hardly see, I cannot walk at all, and many of you can hardly cope with life. What is crucial to remember is this—we don't need just our eyes, just our legs, or just our minds. All we need are the wings of our souls and together we can fly."

7. **Adopt the mindset builders.**
As you avoid thought patterns that can destroy your mindset, you should also adopt ways of thinking that will build it. I call these "mindset builders."

Gratitude

If you are thankful for what you have, you have a head start on a good mindset. Gratitude builds a good mindset.

Faith

You can always draw on the Lord's reliable and dependable strength. Your faith in Him is critical to your mindset.

Humility

Humility is your ability to see yourself in the light of who God is. It gives you the right perspective and restrains you from straying into pride.

Graciousness

Graciousness means that you treat people better than they deserve. Are you the kind of person who always deals with people based on how they treat you? Graciousness treats others according to the Golden Rule, regardless of the way they act toward you.

Respect

Respect is deferential esteem given to others. The Bible teaches us to respect our parents, elders, leaders, and other people.

Servanthood

Don't live for others to serve you; instead, serve others the way Jesus did. Jesus humbled Himself and took the form of a servant (see Philippians 2:8).

Contentment

You may want more, but until you get more—or even if you don't—be thankful for what you have. Contentment means that you do not need to have more to be happy. Happiness is a choice. Choose to be happy with what you have.

CONSTRUCTIVE CRITICISM FOR THE PREPROGRAMMED MINDSET

Ready

> He whose ear listens to the lifegiving reproof will dwell among the wise. He who neglects discipline despises himself, but he who listens to reproof acquires understanding. (Proverbs 15:31–32 NASB)

Set

One of the coach's toughest jobs is telling athletes what they are doing wrong. Most coaches try to do it constructively, but even then many athletes will choose to ignore the instruction or make excuses, blaming everyone else for the problems they themselves have caused.

I was reminded of my imperfections through constructive criticism. It was a painful bullet that shattered my ego. But we all need correction and people who will speak truths to us. My college football coach in California saw so much potential in me to be a great linebacker. But he did not give me the starting job because of that potential. He wanted me to truly earn it. He knew that I was better than the linebacker who was the current starter, and wanted me to start over him, but needed me to mentally do it first. He shared two things with me that has changed my life forever and has allowed me to get a glimpse of my dream in playing professional football. The first was that I would never be the great linebacker I was designed to be while giving 100 percent. That sounds crazy, right? We all are led to believe that 100 percent is the ultimate percentage, but what he allowed me to understand was that although I was giving 100 percent, I had way more to give. I had given 100 percent of my body, but did I give 100 percent of my mind? Did I give 100 percent of my heart? Did I give 100 percent of my will? When you add those up, it is far greater than 100 percent.

The second was for me to speak less and listen more. In my early years, I spoke a little too much. So much so, that it became way too much, because sometimes the talking wasn't necessary. In James 1:19 the writer says: "So then, my beloved brethren, let every man be swift to hear, slow to speak, slow to wrath." Those were some extremely valuable lessons that has catapulted me to a life of success.

Although we seldom ignore corrections, we must respond appropriately to them. Many of us choose to take criticism personally, and that holds us back from making the necessary adjustment required for success. Those of us who accept this type of correction and react accordingly will undoubtedly be better off.

I have seen several athletes handle constructive criticism poorly, and it has ruined many promising careers. I would have to plead guilty to not taking criticism the right way. But Christ wants to speak truth into our lives, many times in the form of the Holy Spirit's constructive criticism.

Again, we have a choice to respond positively or make it personal. The Lord knows that this criticism is for our own good, and when we realize this truth, our relationship with Him deepens. We need to remember that most people who offer constructive criticism are trying to help us. They are trying to get us to become retrofit.

Words of encouragement should prod us on to a greater life in Christ, not lead to the bitterness of spirit that brings glory to Satan and his troops. So the next time someone gives you constructive criticism, just say, "Thanks for caring enough to tell me what was on your heart."

Go

1. How do you handle constructive criticism?
2. Do you try to make yourself feel better by finding faults in the messenger?
3. How can you respond properly to constructive criticism?

Workout

Proverbs 10:17; Proverbs 12:1; Proverbs 15; Hebrews 12:4–11

1. Based on these scriptures, what are three ways to properly handle constructive criticism?
2. How do these scriptures help your response when given constructive criticism?

Overtime

God, I know that I need to be open to instructions from my coaches, my parents, my coworkers, and friends if I am going to be a successful person. I don't want to be limited by my pride. Adjust my preprogrammed mindset and help me as I work to receive instruction with an open heart. Amen.

3

BECAUSE I'M WORTH IT

Have you ever wondered what would be considered a good price for a human being? Yes, how much are you and I worth? Google has records of the net worth of some rich and famous people, but does that sum up our true worth? Sure, they may be worth millions, billions, or even trillions of dollars. I have developed the understanding that they are not worth that much, but their talents, skills, and gifts are. So we are back to the same question: how much are human beings worth?

History has made us believe that there could be a price for human beings. Slavery was one of the most horrific things that has taken place within the shores of our great country. Africans were taken from their land of origin to America and were sold as slaves. This made us the African Americans that we are today. Buying and selling the life of an African American for cheap or premium prices. The slave owners believed that they could buy another human being for the price they were willing to pay in order to get things done.

"I will buy that black person for one hundred dollars," some would say as they attempted to make their purchase of another human being. They believed that human was only worth one hundred dollars in paper money. Thankfully, our country and much of the world today have evolved. But even today, we are still plagued by this ridiculous point of view. One of the most barbaric and inhumane issues that is happening in our world today is the problem of sex trafficking and child sex trafficking.

Not only are adults being trafficked, the rate at which children are involved is even higher. Children are kidnapped and sold as if they are worth nothing more than someone's toy. The value of human life has drastically dropped and has rapidly declined for decades. The rate of abortion is on the incline because many people have been deceived to believe that a conceived child is not an actual child, nothing other than a small thought.

Women, young and old, are being tricked to believe that bringing a life into the world is not worth it. This is a lie because every life has an indescribable worth. This premise for abortion is false and baseless. My beautiful mother conceived me at the tender age of fourteen. I am sure she was bombarded with the thoughts of aborting her baby boy, but because of her love and understanding that I am valuable, she pressed on into motherhood. She placed a premium price on a well-deserving life, for which I am forever grateful. Thank you, Mom!

What about Joseph? His story emphasizes both the assumed and the actual worth of God's most extraordinary creature— the human being. Although his brothers maliciously sold him for twenty shekels of silver, his inexplicable worth was revealed in Egypt. A piece of advice he gave King Pharaoh enriched the king and saved many nations from famine.

In Genesis 37–39, we learn how Joseph was betrayed by his brothers, who were angry with him because he was given a dream from God that foretold how he would rule over them and their father. His brothers were jealous and upset with the thought of Joseph ruling over them, so they plotted to kill him. Instead, they threw him away into a ditch as if he was just a piece of trash. Later, when the Midianite traders passed by, his brothers pulled Joseph up and lifted him out of the pit and sold him to the Midianites for twenty shekels of silver. And they took Joseph to Egypt.

Human trafficking has been happening for centuries. People have been bought and sold and treated as if they are nothing but a possession. This is not because Joseph, trafficked people, or those aborted babies are not valuable, but because society has trained us to believe that there is a price tag on human life. Here is the truth: human beings are infinitely valuable and priceless.

We have more worth than we can ever fathom. The problem is that we believe our worth stems from our gifts, talents, and intellect. Do those things we possess hold value? Absolutely! But that cannot and will never change our true value as a people. No longer should you believe that you are worth what's in your bank account or your level of performance in a sport. Now is the time for you to begin to walk around with your head held high. Hold yourself in high regard, because you are worth more than what anyone could offer. If this were not true, then what I am about to tell you would not have happened.

The most life-changing story that was ever told to me is one that is still changing lives today. Long ago, as the world continued to develop, the divine Creator intervened at the perfect moment to save mankind from the destructive path. Some call Him the divine Creator, but I call Him Father God.

Father God sent His express image, who is 100 percent God, to live as 100 percent man. He did this through a virgin birth; God made this unspeakable miracle happen through His great power. Consequently, the virgin gave birth to one of the Godhead, who also doubles as the son of man. He grew just like us and was dependent on His mother during His developing years.

At age thirty, He began His ministry. The Bible records the purpose of His ministry according to Luke 4:18:

> The Spirit of the Lord is upon Me, because He has anointed Me to preach the gospel to the poor; He has sent Me to heal the brokenhearted, to proclaim liberty to the captives and recovery of sight to the blind, to set at liberty those who are oppressed; to proclaim the acceptable year of the Lord.

This description and references expressly point to Jesus, the only Savior of the world—all who believe in Him. He is the only sinless and blameless human. He voluntarily took the place of sinners and died for their sins on the cross of Calvary. In the process, He suffered punishment meant for us, shed His blood for our remission, and was buried, but physically rose again on the third day. Consequently, He restored what was once a life of destruction for all and converted it into a life of love, peace, and eternal bliss for believers. Thus, the scripture emphasized what we are to Jesus.

You're worth it because:
God knows you, loves you, and has a great plan for you.

Our best plan is inferior to the glorious set of plans God has for us.

> For I know the plans that I have for you; declares the Lord, plans for welfare and not for calamity

to give you a future and a hope. (Jeremiah 29:11 NASB)

God turns bad around for good.

God has unparalleled mastery in turning your mistakes and unpleasant occurrences into jaw-dropping testimonies and miracles. Apostle Paul said:

> And we know that God causes all things to work together for good to those who love God, to those who are called according to His purpose. (Romans 8:28 NASB)

Nothing is impossible for God.

God is the creator of everything; therefore, the greatest giant and mountain are nothing but mere wax to Him—nothing is impossible for Him to do.
But He said:

> The things that are impossible with people are possible with God. (Luke 18:27 NASB)

Jesus has authority over the enemy.

> Behold, I have given you authority to tread on serpents and scorpions, and over all the power of the enemy, and nothing will injure you. (Luke 10:19 NASB)

Jesus paid for your sins.

Jesus paid the supreme price for our sins and curses on the cross of Calvary.

> Surely our griefs He Himself bore, and our sorrows He carried; Yet we ourselves esteemed Him stricken, Smitten of God, and afflicted. But He was pierced through for our transgressions, He was crushed for our iniquities; The chastening for our well-being fell upon Him, and by His scourging we are healed. (Isaiah 53:4–5 NASB)

Jesus defeated death and hell.

God raised Jesus from the dead, and now He sits at the right hand of the Father in heaven as our high priest, intercessor, and advocate.

> Who is the one who condems? Christ Jesus is He who died, yes, rather who was raised, who is at the right hand of God, who also intercedes for us. (Romans 8:34 NASB)

Jesus cares about everything in your life, and no circumstance can change His love for you. He waits for you to adopt an attitude of faith, trust, and obedience to access all His incredible blessings.

> For God so loved the world, that He gave His only begotten Son, that whoever believes in Him shall not perish, but have eternal life. (John 3:16 NASB)

God's unequaled love predates our birth and repentance. He saw more value in us than we know of ourselves. You are worth more than any known treasure.

Without God, you're nothing

Judging the world's four standards of success—money, looks, power, and popularity—none of them are intrinsically bad or evil. In fact, we can use any of them righteously. However, you could have all four of them and still be a complete failure.

None of the four standards address your spiritual life because the world does not have a spiritual measure of success. The world strives after all these things hoping to gain success.

You can have them all and yet fail in God's eyes because they are not His definition of success. One of the best examples of how God views these four standards of success can be seen in the life of King Solomon, the son of David and Bathsheba.

Solomon became the richest, wisest, and most powerful man in the world. Solomon's wealth was indescribable, and only Jesus surpassed Solomon's wisdom.

> So, King Solomon became greater than all the kings of the eath in riches and in wisdom. (1 Kings 10:23 NASB).

Judging by the world's standards, Solomon met all expectations. Then, however, a problem arose:

> Now King Solomon loved many foreign women along with the daughter of Pharaoh. Moabite, Ammonite, Edomite, Sidonian, and Hittite women, from the nations concerning which the Lord had said to the sons of Israel, "You shall not

associate with them, nor shall they associate with you, for they will surely turn your heart away after their gods." Solomon held fast to these in love. He had seven hundred wives, princesses, and three hundred concubines, and his wives turned his heart away. For when Solomon was old, his wives turned his heart away after other gods; and his heart was not wholly devoted to the Lord his God, as the heart of David his father had been. For Solomon went after Ashtoreth the goddess of the Sidonians and after Milcom the detestable idol of the Ammonites. Solomon did what was evil in the sight of the Lord, and did not follow the Lord fully, as David his father had done. Then Solomon built a high place for Chemosh the detestable idol of Moab, on the mountain which is east of Jerusalem, and for Molech the detestable idol of the sons of Ammon. Thus also he did for all his foreign wives, who burned incense and sacrificed to their gods. Now the Lord was angry with Solomon because his heart was turned away from the Lord, the God of Israel, who had appeared to him twice, and had commanded him concerning this thing, that he should not go after other gods; but he did not observe what the Lord had commanded. (1 Kings 11:1-10 NASB)

God appeared to Solomon on two occasions and made him the richest and wisest man on the earth. Consequently, King Solomon wrote the book of Proverbs. However, God had earlier instructed the children of Israel never to intermarry with unbelievers. Evidently, Solomon disobeyed God by marrying several foreign women, thereby lusting after their gods.

God forbade him from marrying foreign wives like other kings of his days. Other kings married foreign wives because potential enemies would have grandchildren in the king's house, preventing them from attacking. In other words, foreign wives were an instrument of peace—and compromise.

Solomon went even further in his disobedience by building monuments and a place of worship for their gods. Kindly pause and consider this level of rebellion. He used the wealth that God had given him to build altars for these women's strange gods. Many of the Canaanite people worshipped Ashtoreth, a goddess of sex, fertility, and war. This worship includes temple prostitution and other sexual perversions.

The Moabites and Ammonites worship Milcom, Chemosh, and Molech, all of whom require babies to be used as sacrifices by killing them on altars and throwing them in fire.

This method of child sacrifice is the Old Testament's version of abortion. Since they did not have the medical technology to abort effectively in the womb, these people simply waited until the babies were born. At other times they waited until a child turned two or three. If they did not like their children, they offered them up to Molech.

The scream of dying children echoed daily from the valley east of Jerusalem where these temples stood. The anger of the Lord burned against Solomon, even though he possessed all four of the world's standards of success, and he died a failure. Unless we want to suffer the same fate, we must seek success in a godly manner.

Again, there is nothing wrong with these four standards. All of us can use them in positive ways. I hold nothing against them, except this: I do not want to be successful in the eyes of the world yet have the anger of the Lord burn against me.

It is unwise to pursue these mundane things, only to discover in eternity that I failed by trying to succeed on earthly standards. Jesus Christ, our perfect example, did not meet many of these standards during His earthly ministry.

For a short time during Jesus's ministry, He was popular; the crowds followed Him. However, the crowds also unanimously echoed a wicked plea against Him—crucify Him! Jesus never gained favor with the authorities, either.

Jesus didn't have strength and security by the world's standards. The soldiers took Him, and He offered no resistance.

Isaiah says Jesus was nothing to look at, that we should gaze upon Him (Isaiah 53). Especially during the period of His trial, He lost every form of attraction.

Certainly, Jesus never had financial wealth. He died penniless, and they buried Him in a borrowed grave. In spite of all these "shortcomings," our Savior was the most successful person who ever lived. No one will ever have the magnitude of success of our Lord Jesus Christ.

However, in the world's eyes, He was a failure. Conversely, King Solomon, who had everything obtainable on earth, died a failure. The comparison between these two men should cause you to question your views about success and the way you live your life.

WHAT MAKES YOU WORTH IT?

Ready

> Brethren I do not regard myself as having laid
> hold of it yet, but one thing I do: forgetting

what lies behind and reaching forward to what lies ahead, I press on toward the goal for the prize of the upward call of God in Christ Jesus. (Philippians 3:13–14 NASB)

Set

Paul uses the phrase "one thing" to bring focus and clarity to his calling. This phrase appears five times in the New International Version of the Bible—once in the verse above in Philippians and four times in the Gospels:

- In Luke 10:42, Jesus says to Martha: "only one thing is needed."
- In both Luke 18:22 and Mark 10:21, Jesus tells the rich man that he still lacks "one thing."
- In John 9:25, the blind man who was healed by Christ tells the Pharisees: "One thing I do know. I was blind but now I see!"

As competitors, ministers, workers, sons, or daughters for Christ, the one thing that God desires is for us to focus on Him.

There is a great organization that understands this great importance of keeping our focus on Him.

The FCA (Fellowship Christian Athletes) Competitor's Creed states: "I am a competitor now and forever. I am made to strive, to strain, to stretch and to succeed in the arena of competition. I am a Christian Competitor and as such, I face my challenger with the face of Christ."

"The "one thing" that we need to focus on as competitors for Christ is the fact that we have been created in the likeness of God Almighty to bring glory to Him everywhere we find ourselves. Anything else takes our focus off the master." (Dan Britton).

Go

1. In your everyday life, what makes it hard for you to keep your focus?
2. As you examine your walk with the Lord, what is the "one thing" that prevents you from keeping your focus on the Lord?
3. What would you describe as the "one thing" on which the Lord wants you to focus?

Workout

Luke 10:38–42; Luke18:18–30; John 9:13–34

1. Based on these scriptures, how can you truly discover worth?
2. What are your thoughts? What will help you live with more understanding of your self-worth, focusing on yourself or focusing on Christ? Why?

Overtime

Lord, there are so many things that take my focus from You. Please forgive me for those times when I have not fixed my eyes on You. Help me, Lord, to focus on You alone. I desire to glorify You in all that I do. Amen.

4

THE JOURNEY:
WHO'S WITH ME?

Life is by far the most amazing, adventurous journey. There are several scintillating events that culminate into the ultimate journey of life. Many of us will experience thousands of stimuli while embarking on this journey; the excitement we feel when our expectations are met or the pains of disappointment; the sadness we feel when someone passes away; the loss of a pet, or the collapse of a relationship; the pain we feel while training to become the best in a competition, or the pain we feel from breaking a bone. I think it is safe to say that the journey of life is truly one of many stimuli.

Many strong-willed individuals would attempt to claim that they are self-made men and women, but nothing can be farther from the truth. Our climb to the top of the mountain cannot be done alone, but with those who have been with you along the journey. Some people are necessary for the whole journey, and some are necessary for few miles, but needless to say, humans are not crafted to be self-made. I have felt alone in many aspects of my life's journey, but later learned that was not true.

Some may argue that at the point of conception is the only time in your life you are alone in your life's journey. This is simply fallacious, because the Bible tells us that God the Father knew us and was there from the beginning of our lives.

> Before I formed you in the womb I knew you.
> (Jeremiah 1:5 NASB)

Before the miracle of pregnancy ever happened, you were known and formed by the Creator before manifesting on earth. No living mammal has ever been born without their mother delivering them through labor. My journey to becoming retrofit has been and still is one that has involved many on the journey.

What about you? Can you think of any? Many of us go through a dangerous phase in life where we are tricked into believing that we are all alone and no one has ever cared for us. This phase leads to heaviness and depression. This can send anyone on a downward spiral, far from the place of recovery, and may consequently lead to suicide.

Here is the truth. There are more people for you than you know. You just have to open your eyes. "I'll be right back, Grandma," said the young man who had just lost his grandfather about a month ago. Where could he be going at 8 p.m. on a Thursday evening?

The young man's grandfather was his hero; he had taught him many things, and played a pivotal role in shaping who the young man was becoming. The young man had earned many accolades and was eager to share them with his grandfather, as he knew that his grandfather would be very proud of him.

One day the young man was wondering why he haven't seen his grandfather for a few days. He was told that he was in the hospital. Confident that his grandfather would be home soon, the young man waited to share the good news with him. After a week, his grandfather still did not show up, and now, the young man got worried. He asked to see his grandfather, and when he did, the truth was revealed to him. "Your grandfather has lung cancer," said his mother.

Not knowing what lung cancer was, he knew that he would see his grandfather soon. So he continued to wait to tell him the good news to his hero. Amazingly, on October 31, the young man got the official news that he was the first player in the past two decades to become first team all- conference mid football season as a sophomore in high school. He was eager to tell his grandfather, as he believed that he would be home before he got there.

After two hours of waiting, he finally called to see if anyone was coming to get him. His aunt broke the bad news to him. "Grandpa is dead," she said. The young man became completely depressed and would not eat for weeks.

Precisely a month later, it was a dark Thursday evening. With a smile on his face to disguise the pain and hurt that lingered inside him, the young man told his grandmother that he would be right back.

The young man grabbed his car keys. He was completely convinced and ready to go through with his plan of embarking on a trip he would never return from. Completely depressed, and ready to end it all, he said goodbye to his grandmother.

"Are you OK?" she asked. "Yes," said the young man. She persistently asked the young man if he was OK. Getting halfway down the stairs and then being asked to come back up to ask the same question, "Are you ok?" This went on 7 times. Finally, by that seventh time she asked him to come up the stairs to ask the same question he broke down in tears. If it were not for the grandmother, he would not be alive today. He felt alone, abandoned, depressed, and utterly drained of life, but his grandmother was there on his journey. This young man was not alone, but all he needed to do was open his eyes.

People who persistently stand by us are those who are genuinely there for us. Along our life's journey, many people have helped and guided us, and some of them are still there today. The loving discipline that we received while growing up has greatly helped our development.

Some loved ones provided the stability that many of us could not create for ourselves. They helped fill the void when you lost someone. They are your positive role models, who helped you develop into the upright young man or woman you are today.

More importantly, the ultimate one who is ever-present to help along your life's journey is the one who has given us hope to live—Jesus Christ, the giver of eternal life. He has promised to be with you even to the end of the earth. When the great confusion blows upon you, remember this truth: we are never alone.

YOU'RE WORTH IT, JUST LEAN ON HIM

Ready

Trust in the Lord forever, for in God the Lord, we have an everlasting Rock. (Isaiah 26:4 NASB)

Set

In 1992, the Olympic Games were held in Barcelona, Spain. Athletes from around the world gathered as they do every four years to compete against the best from every country.

One such athlete was Derek Redmond. Representing England in the 400-meter, Redmond was considered a medal contender—until his semifinal heat.

The crowd in the packed stadium anticipated a great race from this champion runner. The race was moving along well with Redmond in the lead until halfway down the backstretch, when he collapsed on the track with a pulled hamstring. As medical staff rushed toward him, Redmond struggled to get to his feet. He had only one thing on his mind—finishing the race. In severe pain, Redmond made his way down the homestretch and was greeted by his father. With tears in his eyes, his father said, "Son, you do not have to do this." But the younger Redmond said that he had to finish the race.

"Then lean on me," his loving father responded, "and we will finish this together." Staying in their lane to the end, the father and son finished the race. Seeing his son's pain caused Redmond's father to do all he could to help his child. He knew that his son could not finish the race without him. God does the same with us. Through our prayers and petitions, when things get tough, God says, "I will help you finish! Lean on Me and I will see you through to the end."

There are many battles in life that you will not be able to handle on your own, so learn how to lean on the Father. Just as Redmond's father went to him in his time of need, so your heavenly Father will come to you when you call on Him. When He comes to pull you through, swallow your pride and lean on Him. It is only through Christ that can we reach the finish line.

—Jere Johnson

Go

1. Are you broken and alone? Where and what do you turn to fill the void of being alone? Will you lean on Christ to help you through? How and why?
2. How can you lean on Christ to the place of victory?
3. Who is someone that you can lean on today, and why?

Workout

Psalm 30; Psalm 40; Matthew 5:3–4

1. Based on Psalm 30 and 40, what are the takeaways you can gain from David in recognizing that the Lord has never left you?
2. What does the writer in Matthew 5 say that you are when you are poor in spirit and mourning? How does that make you feel, and how can you live out this feeling with the knowledge you learned from Matthew 5?

Overtime

Father, thank You for always being there for me. You will always see me through to the end—I am never alone. Thank You for letting me lean on You at all times!

5

THE APPLICATION PROCESS

"Don't stop." "Don't quit." "Keep pushing," These are some of the phrases we say to ourselves or other people to encourage them. Imagine if you wanted to go to a specific destination and you needed directions. Someone helped you with the directions. Now, it is completely up to you to follow the directions, right?

The choice is completely yours; you can choose to follow the directions or act otherwise. Many people would strictly follow the directions that were given to them and would get there exactly at the time they were told they would arrive.

They may even discover that everything they were told would happen and experience along the way did happen. There are also many people who would choose to partially follow the directions or opt for a shortcut heading toward their destination. They may still arrive at their destination. But it became apparent that although it took them less time, they gained fewer experiences along the way. So rather than follow instructions, they chose a different path and arrived earlier but empty. Unbeknownst to them, fulfillment is not about the destination but the processes of the journey.

Rewards that lack fulfillment are just useless trophies.

There will be times when you adhere strictly to instructions and your journey in the "application process" looks dark, scary, and hopeless. But it is very important for you to know that those dark, scary, and hopeless situations are the supreme opportunities to develop you and make your journey and arrival sweet, impactful, and memorable. So, you cannot give up—you must not give up.

Don't just take my word for it. Scripture reveals how a young man along his journey had some run-ins with some very dark, scary, and hopeless situations. His name was Joseph. His brothers hated him because he was his father's favorite.

One day, Joseph was given a glimpse of his reward in a dream from God, highlighting how he would one day become ruler over his brothers and father. Without thinking, Joseph told his brothers about his dream. First, his father rebuked him. Then his brothers hated him. They considered the option of killing him before selling him to slavery. Joseph had received a glimpse of his reward from God through a dream, but the destination seemed unrealistic because of the negative experience he was having. How can a slave become a ruler over his family?

His predicament did not stop him. He learned from his situation, applied these lessons, and began to live out his life. This was the road that would make the dream God showed him come true. Along this road Joseph pleased God, maximized opportunities, developed integrity, and grew spiritually.

As a slave, he became the deputy of the most powerful leader and nation on earth at that time. Then, a famine hit Egypt as well as the surrounding countries. Before the famine, Joseph had properly prepared more than enough food to feed Egypt and those countries.

It was during this time that Joseph finally reached his destination. The dream that God had showed him before he was sold into slavery came to fruition. Joseph's family was affected by the famine that ravaged Egypt and its neighbors. So when they ran out of food, they came to Egypt to buy food. Guess what? Joseph was in charge of Egypt's food bank. Immediately, they bowed to him, not realizing that it was Joseph. He then revealed his identity and forgave his brothers for their wrongdoing.

> Now do not be grieved or angry with yourselves, because you sold me here, for God sent me before you to preserve life; Now, therefore, it was not you who sent me here, but God. (Genesis 45:5, 8 NASB)

Going through the application process and not skipping one step becomes a beautiful opportunity to develop and understand why the road to your destination turned out the way it did. God wittingly protected Joseph from the hatred and resentment. When he had received understanding of his life's journey, it was easy for him to forgive and comfort his brothers while in his new place of power instead of using his political might to arrest, prosecute, and eliminate them.

Success is not a sudden event; you must learn how to apply, walk, and arrive. Failure to do this will set the wrong standards for success. Desiring success without appreciating and submitting oneself to the process of achieving success can be disastrous.

A FLAWED SENSE OF SUCCESS OR FAILURE

The wrong standards for success will give you a false sense of success or failure. Some people consider themselves successful, but in God's eyes they're wretched, poor, and blantant failures. On the other hand, you may think of yourself as a failure when, in fact, you are highly successful (even if you don't realize it). You have a flawed sense of success or failure because you use the wrong standards to judge. Judge by your own personal growth and not what has been grown around you. If not, you will get caught up in what's around you as a means of success instead of realizing that where you are is not where you once were.

WRONG PARENTING AND MODELING

Another result of having the wrong standards for success is that you will parent and model the wrong principles to your children. After all, they depend on your example and imitate your lifestyle.

Some parents have adopted the wrong standards of success. They teach their children to be busy with school, sports, and friends, but God comes last on their list of priorities. When you raise your children that way, they grow up and nurture their children the same way.

We must teach our children that God is first, period! God and the church are primary and we must not sacrifice our time with Him for anything. Remember, those four standards of worldly success do not contain a spiritual element. So if we parent based on worldly values, our children will grow up thinking of success in those terms.

It becomes imperative for us to raise our children to love and put God first. Then other things follow. If you can successfully train your children to love, serve, and prioritize God, they will succeed in life.

WRONG DECISION MAKING

If you have the wrong standards for success, it will affect your decision-making process and outcome. Sometimes when I speak to young people I love saying, "Choose a career that fills your heart first and your pocketbook second."

Some important and valuable people in this society are not paid enough and never will be—police officers, firefighters, teachers, and others. Military officers do what they do because they simply have a calling to do it.

They are sacrificing wealth for the sake of doing what they love—a great sacrifice. If you are making a lot of money in your chosen career, that is awesome. God might have called you to do that. However, I strongly advise that you don't choose a job solely for its financial gain.

LACK OF INNER FULFILLMENT

Lack of inner fulfillment is another problem that comes from having the wrong standards of success. This experience happens so often in people's lives. You may do everything the world prescribes for achieving success, yet, deep down in your heart, you know something is missing. Your heart is simply alerting you that you are on the wrong path.

NOT ACCOMPLISHING GOD'S BEST

It is impossible to use the wrong standards of success and fulfill God's best for your life. King Solomon died a failure; he did not finish well. Why did this happen? He conformed to worldly standards and strayed out of God's commandment. Remember, the apostle Paul warns us not to be conformed to this world, but to be transformed by renewing our minds (see Romans 12:2).

At first, King Solomon strictly adhered to God's commandments and kept His precepts. As the wisest man, he wrote the book of Proverbs, expounding on morals, speech, and money—including everything that's important in life. He was able to write Proverbs because God had transformed his mind to think like God. Later, Solomon's foreign wives lured him to a worldly way of thinking. If you want true success, and to truly be retrofit you must follow God's definition and not the world's standards during the application process.

OBSTACLES AND OPPORTUNITIES: TIME FOR THE APPLICATION PROCESS

Ready

> "Send out for yourself men so that they may spy out the land of Canaan, which I am going to give to the sons of Israel; you shall send a man from each of their fathers' tribes, everyone a leader among them." So Moses sent them from the wilderness of Paran at the command of the Lord, all of them men who were heads of the sons of Israel. (Numbers 13:2–3 NASB)

Set

When you walk onto a court to play a game, do you immediately think that you're going to lose or win? Do you stare at your opponents while they warm up and begin to wonder why you even laced up your Nikes, or do you focus on giving your all? Do you see obstacles, or do you see opportunities?

In Numbers 13, the spies were sent into Canaan to check out the land. God had already given them great victories in battle and rescued them from tough situations. During the forty-day mission, they could have seen great opportunities, but they didn't.

Only two guys, Joshua and Caleb, thought that they could succeed in acquiring the land. The rest of the team did what I think many of us would have done. They saw a wall and a formidable opponent and said, "We don't think that we can do this!"

Well, that is true because we can't, but God can. It's strange that the Israelites didn't remember the situations from which God had delivered them and the victories they had enjoyed. They also forgot that God had commanded them to go into the land and that He had promised to give it to them. These were His words: "Send some men to explore the land of Canaan, which I am giving to the Israelites."

God has already given us assurance of victory. We only need to receive what He has promised. We are so much like these Israelites when faced with challenging situations. But I pray we become more like Joshua and Caleb, who received and believed in the opportunity that God had given them.

Go

1. When you compete, or in everyday life, what obstacles do you see?
2. With God's help, how might these obstacles be turned into opportunities?
3. What practical steps can you take to increase your faith in God's plan for your life?

Workout

Numbers 13:26–30; Deuteronomy 31:8; 2 Corinthians 12:9

1. After reading these scriptures and understanding truly how great God is, what obsticles can you turn into opportunities?
2. What are two opportunities in your life right now that you can see through with faith?

Overtime

Lord, help me to remember that through my doubt, I can see only obstacles. But through my faith in You, I can see opportunities. Allow me to increase this faith every day. Amen.

CHAPTER

6

ETERNAL PRINCIPLES

According to Stephen Covey, there are three constants in life: change, choice, and principles. Making changes and proper choices can be great, but living life by principles can bring change and help with making appropriate choices. Many today would argue that they would choose a life lived with good morals over principles, but what happens when those morals are challenged? Without the principles to back them up, those morals can easily be defeated.

There are many places to receive good and wholesome principles. The first place is the home—charity begins at home. It is not unusual for parents to assiduously instill principles in their children, to guide and help them as they grow and develop. School is another place that attempts to instill principles in children through different methods. They teach English, writing, math, and other subjects in a principle-centered way. Take math for instance. When teaching an equation, teachers emphasize foundational systems on how to solve the equation. That should help us get to the next academic level, at least in math. In any system known to humans, there are always foundational principles for a system of belief, behavior, or for a chain of reasoning. The way and pattern of doing things stems from the foundational standpoint. So I ask: what is the foundation upon which you stand, and how is it important to you?

As you would expect, a foundation is the most important part of any structure, and the strength and design of the foundation is more critical than the eventual structure. Some people build their foundation on things, ideas, habits and other unstable parameters. I call this the "sinking-sand foundation." As nice as it is to build a magnificent house on the beach, what will you do if that beach is affected by a tsunami or rainstorm?

A sinking-sand foundation can lead to extreme damage and even in some cases complete destruction. Those who choose to live their lives based on a foundation like this may think that what they believe in can stabilize them enough not to fall off the cliff. But it will surely fall apart. Jesus's teaching about the sinking-sand foundation thousands of years ago is still relevant and applicable today.

> Everyone who hears these words of Mine and does not act on them, will be like a foolish man who built his house on the sand. The rain fell, and the floods came, and the winds blew and slammed against that house; and it fell—and great was its fall. (Matthew 7:26 NASB)

Notice that this sinking-sand foundation failed because it was movable. It lacked rigidity, strength, and stability. When water hits sand it washes away, but when water hits a rock, the rock remains intact. It is very important for us to build our lives upon a solid foundation that is immoveable. No matter who you are, life will happen to you, and the foundation upon which you have built your house will be greatly tested. I am confident of this truth: a life that is founded on an intimate relationship with Jesus Christ will stand the test of time, trials, and tribulations. There was a time where the foundation of my life was built on sinking sand. Like everyone who has ever been created, God has given me gifts and talents, and I thought I should build my foundation upon these things. The talent to play sports such as football. The talent to speak well. My charisma. Believing that all these things would be able to build a solid foundation, only to find out I was highly mistaken. None of these are sustainable. What if I got injured? There goes that part of my foundation, completely washed away like sand. What if my ability to speak well reaches a plateau, and no one wants to hear me anymore? Or, worse, my speech wasn't all that great in the first place. There goes another part of my foundation, washed away like sand. What if my charisma is not all that compelling, and I have not truly inspired anyone? Once again, there goes another piece of my foundation, washed away like sand.

Being retrofit places a strong emphasis and importance on the foundation. Since principles are foundational, here are ten strong principles to build your personal life upon.

PRINCIPLE ONE

Know what you are to know who you are.

In order to undertand this principle, you must first understand this extremely important fact: A human is a spirit, has a soul, and lives in a body.

> Now may the God of peace Himself sanctify you entirely; and may your spirit and soul and body be preserved complete, without blame at the coming

of our Lord Jesus Christ. (1 Thessalonians 5:23 NASB)

The fact that human beings are spirits living inside physical bodies is one of the lesser known truths. When Paul wrote to the Thessalonians, he prayed that God should preserve their spirit, soul, and body. A human being is not just a piece of flesh. There is more to human beings than meets the eye. When people speak in a very proud and arrogant way, it is because they are not aware of how real eternal things are. This must be a part of the reasons individuals judge others by their outer appearance.

IS THERE MORE TO THIS LIFE?

Furthermore, we had earthly fathers to discipline us, and we respected them; shall we not much rather be subject to the Father of spirits, and live? (Hebrews 12:9 NASB)

If God is the Father of spirits, then we His children are spirits. This implies that our bodies are just containers of the spirit.

THE BIBLE DESCRIBES THE BODY AS A HOUSE

For we know that if the earthly tent which is our house is torn down, we have a building from God, a house not made with hands, eternal in the heavens. (2 Corinthians 5:1 NASB)

The Bible records that after the death of Lazarus, he was carried by angels into Abraham's bosom.

> Now the poor man died and was carried away
> by the angels to Abraham's bosom; and the
> rich man also died and was buried. (Luke 16:22
> NASB)

My freshman year in high school was one of the toughest years in my life because I lost my grandfather, who was one of my biggest heros other than my mother. I was that young man described a few chapters ago. On that dark and cold October 31st night, I got the call that my grandfather had passed away. Bombarded with depression, desperation, pain, and grief, I just could not understand that he could die at that time in my life. A time where I truly needed some solid male role models in my life, only to have one taken away. I thought it was all over for him. That his story was completely done, and that was it for him. Long forgotten.

Just days later we had the funeral in remembrance of my grandfather. I gazed with complete hurt and grief at my grandfather's casket being lowered into the ground at the grave site. I just could not shake the fact that this was completely it for my grandfather's story. Such a good man, and someone who loved the Lord, who would now sleep forever, never to be thought of again. Another story that has been erased from existence. And then my knowledge of death according to God's way was enlightened. I later began to realize that my grandfather was a modern-day Lazarus. That the gravesite was not the end of his story. I realized that after the body dies, the spirit lives on!

The real Lazarus was carried into Abraham's bosom, while his dead body remained below the earth. Remember the rich man, who had everything in life: wealth, influence, and access to better health care. He also died and was probably given a royal funeral.

Dear friend, the Lazarus who was in Abraham's bosom was the real Lazarus which was his soul and spirit. The rich man who was languishing in hell was not the rich man who had been buried at that lavish funeral. It was the soul and the spirit of the rich man that was being tormented by the fire of hell.

The fleshly remains of human beings stay on earth long after the spirit has departed to a Christ-filled eternity or a Christless eternity. I know that many people are not aware of this great reality, that they are spirit, soul, and body.

YOU ARE MORE THAN A BODY

There are many people who spend much time dressing their bodies, putting on makeup, and even physically training their bodies. Which is totally appropriate. But it is disheartening that many people, both believer and nonbeliever, walk out of the door without even saying a five-minute prayer to the true God, the creator of the cosmos. This is because they are not aware that they are more than a body. They are not conscious that they are spirits living in a body. Hence, they spend all their time on their bodies alone.

People who become conscious of their spirit and soul spend time to build up and develop the spirit. Many governments of nations are not aware that human beings are made up of more than just bodies and minds. They stress education and physical fitness but they leave out the real person. First, humans are spiritual beings—the mind and the body are just mortal accessories of the human spirit.

DEVELOP THE HUMAN SPIRIT

Now is the time for all human beings to be aware of the spirit that dwells in them. It is time for us to develop the human spirit. You can develop your human spirit first and foremost by receiving the gift God has given to us all. This gift is the payment for every sin (an immoral act considered to be a transgression against divine law) and has made us spotless in the sight of God, which rewards us eternal life with Him. The next step to develop the human spirit is by praying. You can also develop your human spirit by being filled with the Holy Spirit of Jesus Christ. He is the very Spirit of God, which produces gifts such as the speaking in tongues and many others.

> One who speaks in a tongue edifies himself; but one who prophesies edifies the church. (1 Corinthians 14:4 NASB)

The Bible says that when you speak in tongues you build up, charge, and edify your spirit. What exercise does to the body, prayer confers the same effect on the human spirit. It is time to become conscious of our spirit and consistently exercise it. You are a tripartite being—possessing spirit, soul, and a body. But what is soul? The Bible makes it clear that the soul is different from the spirit.

> For the word of God is living and active and sharper than any two-edged sword and piercing as far as the division of soul and spirit, of both joints and marrow, and able to judge the thoughts and intentions of the heart. (Hebrews 4:12)

There is a dividing asunder (a demarcation) between the spirit and the soul of a human being. There are many words in the Bible that are used to describe the actions of the soul.

ACTIVITIES OF THE SOUL

Scripture is replete with activities that our soul can carry out:

The soul can rejoice (Psalm 31:7).
The soul can magnify and bless the Lord (Psalm 103:2).
The soul can be downcast (Psalm 42:5).
The soul can be grieved (Judges 10:16).
The soul can be discouraged (Numbers 21:4).
The soul can be joyful (Psalm 35:9).

These are just a few of the emotions that the soul expresses. We can therefore conclude that the soul is the part of the human that experiences thoughts, feelings, and emotions.

THE SOUL LIVES ON

The soul of the rich man was alive in hell, which is why he could remember Lazarus. The rich man thought things were still the same as they used to be. That is why he wanted to send Lazarus an errand—to give him water.

Additionally, the soul of the rich man helped him remember his five brothers. He pleaded with father Abraham to prevent them from coming to join him in hell. He pitied anyone who would ever come to hell.

What did Jesus say about the soul? He said: "For what will it profit a man if he gains the whole world and forfeits his soul?

Or what will a man give in exchange for his soul?" (Matthew 16:26 NASB).

PRINCIPLE TWO

The spirit of an unsaved person is dead and desperately wicked.

> The heart is more deceitful than all else and
> is desperately sick; who can understand it?
> (Jeremiah 17:9 NASB)

When a person is not born again, he has what I call an "unsaved spirit." There are different names the Bible gives unbeliever: sinner, blind, unregenerated, etc.

The Word of God makes it abundantly clear that anyone who is not a believer has an unregenerated spirit and is capable of exhibiting several evil tendencies. Every unsaved person is in a terrible spiritual condition and a potential victim of God's wrath.

> For the wrath of God is revealed from heaven
> against all ungodliness and unrighteousness of
> men who suppress the truth in unrighteousness.
> (Romans 1:18 NASB)

In our contemporary world, the wickedness of men is escalating disturbingly. Many people have forsaken the living God. God has given them up to become dead and darkened in their spirits.

> For even though they knew God, they did not
> honor Him as God or give thanks, but they
> became futile in their speculations, and their

foolish heart was darkened. (Romans 1:21
NASB)

The heart of an unsaved person is darkened and rebrobate.
Furthermore, God has given up on the wicked, so that they may
follow their own desires and perverted feelings.

Therefore, God gave them over in the lusts of
their hearts to impurity, so that their bodies
would be dishonored among them. (Romans
1:24 NASB)

Not only is the spirit of the unsaved person darkened with
death, but the mind of the unsaved person has also degenerated
into a depraved condition.

And just as they did not see fit to acknowledge
God any longer, God gave them over to a
depraved mind, to do those things which are
not proper. (Romans 1:28 NASB)

The subsequent verses highlight the long list of evil
characteristics that unsaved humans exhibit. Their hearts are
filled with every conceivable evil.

Being filled with all unrighteousness,
wickedness, greed, evil; full of envy, murder,
strife, deceit, malice, they are gossips, slanderers,
haters of God, insolent, arrogant, boastful,
inventors of evil, disobedient to parents, without
understanding, untrustworthy, unloving,
unmerciful. (Romans 1:29–31 NASB)

Truthfully, an unsaved spirit is desperately wicked, and this truth is evident in our everyday lives. God has warned Christians against marrying non-Christians because a non-Christian has an unregenerated spirit and is capable of many evil things. One of the major reasons a believer must not be unequally yoked to an unbeliever is this: unbelievers easily break covenants—they are unfaithful. (See Romans 1:31.)

Most unbelievers do not stick to their promises. It is rare to find an unbeliever who is faithful to their marriage covenant. Once upon a time, a man said to me: "I have never seen a faithful unbelieving husband." As I grew up I came to discover that covenant breaking was part and parcel of the unbeliever's lifestyle. They say, "I will" and "I do," but they won't and they don't. Hence, among many other reasons, God commanded that Christians should not marry unbelievers.

Do not think that God is trying to punish you by telling you not to marry an unbeliever. Instead, through this commandment, God is trying to prevent your heart from being broken by a covenant breaker. Do not be deceived by the dignified appearance of the unbeliever.

He or she may be a school prefect, class prefect, minister of state, or even the president. The nature of an unsaved person is described in detail for you in Romans 1:29–31. Folks, believe in the Bible more than you believe your eyes. But, if you were to find yourself in this kind of relationship, there is still hope. Paul writes in 1 Corinthians 7:14—For the unbelieving husband is sanctified through his wife, and the unbelieving wife is sanctified thorugh her believing husband. In this God has extended His grace the one may be won over through the other who is the believer.

By common confession, great is the mystery of godliness. (2 Timothy 3:16 NASB)

Wickedness comes naturally. No one teaches a child to be wicked. This explains why children lie, cheat, and steal without being taught to do so. It is because the unsaved spirit is at work in them. When I was in high school, I couldn't comprehend why God had seemingly given up the human race to its perverted way of life. It is these unsaved and degenerated people of which I am one that Jesus came to the earth to save. Hence, Jesus said a person must be born again. Another term for being born again is regeneration. When you become regenerated, you essentially become changed—the Bible calls you a new creature. God made a new creation out of the old corrupt person.

Naturally, when a spouse dies, there is no way to keep the body at home regardless of how much a husband and wife loved each other. When death lays its icy hands on either partner, they physically part company. The dead body is taken to the mortuary, and subsequently to the grave. Why is this? The person is dead, and the process of decomposition and degeneration commences.

Do you remember what God told Adam and Eve? He said, "In the day that you eat this fruit you will die." Genesis 2:17 NASB. In other words, immediately after Adam and Eve sinned, they died. The condition of spiritual death entered their spirits and there was no way God could be in fellowship with them any more. Consequently, He banished them out of the garden and separated them from Himself, and by extension, the entire human race was separated from God. Amazingly, salvation breaks the wall that separates humans from God.

For He Himself is our peace, who made both groups into one and broke down the barrier of the dividing wall, by abolishing in His flesh the enmity, which is the law of commandments contained in ordinances, so that in Himself He might make the two into one new man, thus establishing peace. (Ephesians 2:14, 16 NASB)

A person is estranged from God before being born again. They may look good on the outside, but they have a corrupt and wicked nature. That is why democracy and rule of law are important. When a person with such nature is vested with power, the tendency to do evil is unlimited. In every nation where there has been a military dictator, inconceivable atrocities have been recorded.

But when a person is in Christ, they are born again. They are regenerated and become a new person. When we speak of being born again, it does not mean returning to your mother's womb. Instead, it is your spirit, the inner nature, that is born again.

That which is born of the flesh is flesh, and that which is born of the Spirit is spirit. (John 3:6 NASB)

If you wash a pig and dress it up with a wedding suit, all you have is a dressed-up pig. You have successfully attended to its body but ignored the root cause responsible for its dirty nature. This same pig will wallow in dirty water at the earliest opportunity. Obeying a set of rules does not change your heart. Coming to Christ and being born again is what affords every person the opportunity to have a new heart.

I believe that it is only a change in the unsaved nature of humans that can bring about the desired change in our world. That can bring one to truly becoming retrofit. New Year's resolutions and obeying rules do not change humans because the spirit of the unsaved man is dead and desperately wicked. No one toys with a dead thing. Dead things must be separated from living things. The only hope for the dead and wicked human spirit is the miracle of rebirth through the finished work of Jesus Christ.

PRINCIPLE THREE

The spirit of a saved person is righteous and truly holy.

> And put on the new self, which in the likeness of God has been created in righteousness and holiness of the truth. (Ephesians 4:24 NASB)

When a person becomes regenerated the spirit within is changed. We have learned earlier that the unsaved spirit is desperately wicked and corrupt. What about the new creation? The new creation is righteous and truly holy!

Scripture makes us know that we are righteous when we become born again. God expects us to put on (act like) the new spirit which is created in righteousness and true holiness. Often, in an attempt to sound humble, we tell the Lord that we are sinners and not worthy to approach His throne. It is time for us to acknowledge what God has done to our hearts because we are the righteousness of God in Christ Jesus.

> He made Him who knew no sin to be sin on our behalf, so that we might become the righteousness of God in Him. (2 Corinthians 5:21 NASB)

If we are the righteousness of God, it means that we cannot be more righteous than we are today. The righteousness of God is the highest form of purity and void of sin.

Somebody once said, "I don't feel any different now that I'm born again!" This is not about feelings but realities that have taken place. Can you feel your liver or your small intestines? Obviously not! But they exist within you. If surgery was performed and your appendix was taken out, the doctors would inform you that they have removed a part of your intestine. You are supposed to accept the new reality that took place in your abdomen during the surgery.

Being born again is a spiritual operation in which God recreates your spirit. He takes out the old, hardened, and depraved spirit and puts in a new and righteous one. When this happens, it becomes expedient for us to acknowledge the good things that are in us because Christ dwells in us as Christians.

We are not supposed to go around saying negative things about ourselves. If you say, "I am not a smart person," you are hurting yourself. If you say "I am a sinner" you are opposing the Word of God. Instead say "I am a sinner who was saved by grace through Grace in Jesus Christ who now has been made to be righteous in Christ." It is time to acknowledge good things about yourself and Christ's finished work.

> Through the knowledge of every good thing which is in you for Christ's sake. (Philemon 6 NASB)

Acknowledging the goodness of Jesus Christ in your life will make your faith come alive. Always say to yourself, *I am the righteousness of God! I'm a new person! I can make it! I am holy!* These confessions will help you live a blameless and victorious life.

Any regenerated Christian who lives in sin is living contrary to his new nature. For such an individual, living in sin becomes a choice because the power of sin and Satan have been broken, and God has endowed such an individual with a new nature. When you are a new creature, it is no longer natural to do evil because it is against your nature as a new creation.

Before you were born again, there are some evil habits and tendencies that you exhibit effortlessly without noticing it. After surrendering your heart to the Lord, an inner witness tells you, *this is wrong! Don't do it!* That is the new person crying out, instructing from within, telling you what to do. The Bible says, "Put on the new self." Ephesians 4:24 NASB. It implies that you should act like a new and regenerated person because God has made you a brand-new being.

You can only increase your faith in your inherited righteousness and display your new nature. When you are conscious of your righteousness in Christ, you will become as bold as a lion.

> The wicked flee when no one is pursuing, But the righteous are bold as a lion. (Proverbs 28:1 NASB)

Through righteousness, you will rule and dominate in the earth as if Satan and his cohort never existed. As you live out this truth, you will overcome your enemies through the gift of righteousness in Christ Jesus! You have the responsibility to stand up and become an overcomer. You are no longer under condemnation because you are the righteousness of God.

> For if by the transgression of the one, death reigned through the one, much more those who receive the abundance of grace and of the gift of

> righteousness will reign in life through the One,
> Jesus Christ. (Romans 5:17 NASB)

PRINCIPLE FOUR

After regeneration, your spirit is a newborn baby, and it must grow.

> Like newborn babies, long for the pure milk of
> the word, so that by it you may grow in respect
> to salvation. (1 Peter 2:2 NASB)

Without any iota of doubt, the salvation of your soul kick-starts a significant change in you. However, we must understand exactly what has happened. A person starts life as a baby and must mature into an adult.

Many times, people have the wrong impression about the Christian faith. The evangelist preaches and says, "Tonight is your night! Your life will never be the same again." He goes on to add, "After tonight, every yoke shall be broken in your life." He declares, "All who are heavy laden must come to Jesus and He will give you rest." This may give the impression that you instantaneously become a mature Christian. But that is not true!

Being born again is just the beginning of a long process. You must go through three important stages of development. Every Christian goes through these three stages whether they know it or not: the baby stage, the childhood stage, and then the mature, adult stage.

PRINCIPLE FIVE

After salvation, your mind is still the same; it must be renewed.

> And do not be conformed to this world, but
> be transformed by the renewing of your mind,
> so that you may prove what the will of God is,
> that which is good and acceptable and perfect.
> (Romans 12:2 NASB)

When you become born again, God gives you a new heart, not a new mind. It is therefore the duty of every Christian to renew their mind. If you do not renew your mind, you will be a new creation but armed with an old mind. There are many Christians who are genuine new creations but still have unrenewed minds.

If you belong to a good church that constantly teaches the Word of God, and you diligently apply every truth being taught, your mind will be renewed. Unfortunately, there are some people who think they know all there is to know in the Word of God.

It is dangerous to stop learning. Don't be tired of learning! Every Christian must decide to remain a diligent learner of the Word of God. Come what may, you must keep learning. You will always discover things that you do not know.

Years ago, I heard a pastor giving a testimony about his life. Before he was saved, he was a pornographer by profession. He acted in pornographic films and posed for pornographic photographs. Sex was his work, and he didn't see anything wrong with it.

He thought he was showing love each time he slept with a girl. This lifestyle of fornication continued after he got born again. He slept with one girl after the other. It never occurred to him that there was something wrong with sleeping with someone you haven't married.

One night, he was in bed with one of the girls when suddenly, a huge black figure appeared at the foot of his bed. He was terrified and thought to himself, *Something is not right!* The next day, he searched his Bible and discovered where the Word of God says fornication is wrong.

> But immorality or any impurity or greed must not even be named among you as is proper among saints. (Ephesians 5:3 NASB)

Believe it or not, this man was born again. But because of his background, he did not even know that fornication was a sin. It could be that because of your background you are not even aware that certain things are sinful.

I know some Christians who are prejudiced or even racist. There are pastors who are racist in their thoughts and decisions. Without even realizing it, we carry on doing wrong things although we are genuinely born again in our hearts. That is why we need the Word of God to renew our minds.

> but be transformed by the renewing of your mind. (Romans 12:2 NASB)

It is actually the renewing of our minds that brings about a visible transformation. If you read the Bible and apply its commandments, your mind will be renewed and your attitude will change. The real change we look for as Christians comes through the renewal of our mind by the Word of God.

There are many Christians who do not give to the Lord simply because their minds are polluted with wrong ideas. Some think the pastors are just using the money for their extravagant lifestyles. However, every Christian who has his mind renewed will find himself being transformed in the area of his finances **and so many other areas.**

HOW TO RENEW YOUR MIND

Let's assume your mind is a computer that has to be programmed. Whatever you feed into the mind is what will come out. Your mind will be renewed by receiving the Word. The old thoughts and ideas will be cleared out as you receive the Word.

> You are already clean because of the word which
> I have spoken to you. (John 15:3 NASB)

Your mind is also renewed by joining the right church and learning godly truths, principles, and precepts. As you receive the Word through your pastor, you will gradually experience a change in your mind.

> So that He might sanctify her, having cleansed
> her by the washing of water with the word.
> (Ephesians 5:26 NASB)

It is the renewed mind that will help you live out the new life. When people see the new life, they instantly know that something significant has happened to you.

PRINCIPLE SIX

After you are saved, your body is still the same; you must keep it under control.

> But I discipline my body and make it my slave,
> so that, after I have preached to others, I myself
> will not be disqualified. (1 Corinthians 9:27
> NASB)

When you are saved, your body is the same old body. Salvation doesn't change your physical body. If you were tall and skinny before salvation, you will remain tall and skinny after salvation. If you had long hair before you were born again, you'll still have long hair after salvation.

Does this mean nothing has happened to you? No! Your spirit is recreated in God. When people give their lives to Christ, they often believe that everything will be different from that moment onward. However, they get home only to realize they still have the old feelings they had before salvation—lust, jealousy, hatred, etc.

The devil begins to tell them, "You are not a real Christian, you are not saved, you are not born again!" Satan continues to harass you by saying, "If you are really born again, such a thought or feeling would never occur to you. None of the Christians sitting in this church has the kind of thoughts you are having."

But Satan is a liar! We all have thoughts and feelings that we don't want to have even though we are born again. Everyone who is born again still has to contend with the flesh. Even Paul was worried about his flesh. He knew that his flesh could disgrace him one day. That is why he kept his flesh under constant control.

> Whoever loves discipline loves knowledge.
> (Proverbs 12:1 NASB)

CONTROL YOUR FLESH

There are practical ways by which you can keep your body under control. First, be aware of the evil tendencies that is in your flesh. Spend time praying and fasting on a regular basis, and do not give opportunities to your flesh. To control the flesh, we need godly wisdom that will help us stay far away from its dangerous enticements.

> Only do not turn your freedom into an opportunity for the flesh (Galatians 5:13 NASB)

If we expose ourselves to certain negative things, we will fall. God's Word says, "Flee youthful lusts." 2 Timothy 2:22. If God knows we could win the fight against fleshly lust by flshly means, He would have told us to fight. When God says run, then, you must run! Don't stand and fight. Don't act like Lot's wife and turn back to your old desires, which got her turned into a pilar of salt; flee for your life! Your body is still the same, so don't trust yourself in this matter. Give no place to the devil and give no opportunity to your flesh.

> And do not give the devil and opportunity (Ephesians 4:27 NASB)

PRINCIPLE SEVEN

After you are born again, your mind is still open to all kinds of thoughts; you must learn to think on the right things.

> We are destroying speculations and every lofty thing raised up against the knowledge of God,

and we are taking every though captive to the
obedience of Christ. (2 Corinthians 10:5 NASB)

You may be a born-again Christian who keeps your body
under subjection. You constantly renew your mind on the Word
of God, but your mind is still open to all kinds of thoughts from
the devil. The devil will always appeal to your mind. The Bible
teaches us that we must cast down imaginations.

Truthfully, your mind is the real battleground where Satan's
most powerful tools, and suggestions, pummels you from
every angle. To conquer this, you must learn how to resist it. A
thought is like a bird that flies over your head. You cannot stop
it from flying but you can stop it from making a nest on your
head. When ungodly thoughts come to you, vehemently resist
and dislodge them.

Don't be surprised when certain things happen to you. That
is the fight of every born-again Christian: to keep your mind
pure at all times. The devil plagues us with thoughts of fear and
worry. During my clinical hours as an EMT at the hospital, I
saw many young patients very sick in hospital beds. Soon, a
spirit of fear oppressed me. I would imagine myself having
some of the same diseases, and I even planned every detail of
my funeral in my mind. Fear is an oppressive spirit that works
through the mind. I had to shake off the fears and anxieties that
were invading my soul.

Whether it is worry, fear, or lust, you must learn to cast
down these imaginations. Capture your thoughts and make
them obedient to the Word of God. Resist the devil by resisting
the thoughts and suggestions that he consistently entices you
with. The Bible admonishes us to think about those things that
are pure, holy, and peaceful.

Finally, brethren, whatever is true, whatever is honorable, whatever is right, whatever is pure, whatever is lovely, whatever is of good repute, if there is any excellence and if anything, worthy of praise, dwell on these things. (Philippians 4:8 NASB)

CONTROL YOUR THOUGHTS

One of the best ways to control your thoughts is to listen to godly teachings and tapes. Additionally, Christian music and videos are good tools to help you saturate your mind with God's Word, thereby controlling your thoughts. In your Christian walk, do not give place to the devil by allowing evil thoughts to settle in your mind. They will oppress and obsess you until you become possessed.

PRINCIPLE EIGHT

You must believe in God to experience the supernatural life.

Jesus said, remove the stone. Martha, the sister of the deceased, said to Him, Lord, by this time there will be a stench, for he has been dead four days. Jesus said to her, Did I not say to you that if you believe, you will see the glory of God? So they removed the stone. Then Jesus raised His eyes, and said, Father, I thank You that You have heard Me. I knew that You always hear Me; but because of the people standing around I said it, so that they may believe that You sent Me. (John 11:39–42 NASB)

If you are to experience the supernatural life, you will have to believe in God. You must believe in the word of God and His voice. It is impossible to experience the supernatural life without having a deep walk with God.

Here is the eternal rule: "If you believe, you will see the glory of God." Personally, in my life and walk with God, I have seen the glory of God because of strong belief in Him. I believe in the call of God and that He has called me to be someone who is to share the light of Christ everywhere I go . I believe that I should give myself wholly to the ministry by abandoning all secular activities and distractions to stay focused on the ministry. I believe God would take care of me as I serve Him.

All these beliefs deepened and enriched my walk with God. I began to see the glory of His provision, church growth, and God began to open the hearts of people to receive the good news of Christ that I would bring. Having tasted the glory of His riches, I'm confident that you will see the glory of God when you believe. However, an unstable and doubting person can never see the glory of God.

PRINCIPLE NINE

You must become obedient to experience the supernatural.

> And Jesus said to her, Women, what does that have to do with us? My hour has not yet come. His mother said to the servants, whatever He says to you, do it. (John 2:4–5 NASB)

In the story of the amazing miracle of turning water into wine, Jesus commanded the servants to pour water into the pitchers. It was Mary, His mother, who gave them the master key for bringing on the supernatural: "Whatever He says to you, do it." If you want to see the supernatural, you must be obedient to the Word of God. I have experienced the supernatural by obeying what God said to me. When he spoke to me and told me to write books, I laughed hysterically, asking *Who would want to read my book?* Eventually, I obeyed, and God has proved His faithfulness again and again.

PRINCIPLE TEN

You must press your way into the supernatural.

> The Law and the Prophets were proclaimed until John; since that time the gospel of the kingdom of God has been preached, and everyone is forcing his way into it. (Luke 16:16 NASB)

After you are born again, you must press your way into the things of God. You will not experience the supernatural power of God unless you press hard to enter. The devil is already agitated and unhappy that you are born again.

He is not going to sheepishly allow you experience more victories. In your quest to progress spiritually, Satan will make things difficult for you. He will *fight you* every step of the way. But press on because you are more than a conqueror.

Laziness, indifference, and laxity will not get you anywhere in the kingdom of God. Make no mistake about it. The law and the prophets were, until John. But now, the kingdom of God has come and everyone must press into it. All those who sit back and think they will be known because they are honest, disobedient Christians do not understand what is happening. Being happy, honest, and sincere is different from pressing hard to enter the kingdom of God and possessing all that belongs to you.

There was a man who was placed by the pool of Bethesda for thirty-eight years. Every time a supernatural miracle was about to occur, another person would press through and enter the water before him.

> The sick man answered Him, Sir, I have no man to put me into the pool when the water is stirred up, but while I am coming, another steps down before me. Jesus said to him, get up, pick up your pallet and walk. Immediately the man became well and picked up his pallet and began to walk. Now it was the Sabbath on that day. (John 5:7–9 NASB)

I have had to fight to be holy which is to be dedicated to God, and spiritual, and to press my way into the things of God. Previously, I had fought to be in full-time ministry, to become a minister of God, to experience His anointing, and to relate with some who are in the ministry. Nothing will be freely given to you on a silver platter. Rise up and press your way into the things of God!

The man by the pool of Bethesda was in the same spot for thirty-eight years. How long do you want to be in the same spot? You have to fight and become aggressive about spiritual things! Be aware that lustful thoughts will not just walk away from you, you must banish them. Do you think that wicked people will just stop following you? Certainly not! You will have to fight your way out and press your way into the kingdom of God.

FOLLOWING PRINCIPLES FOR QUALIFICATION

Ready

> Therefore, I run in such a way, as not without
> aim; I box in such a way, as not beathing the air;
> but I discipline my body and make it my slave,
> so that, after I have preached to others, I myself
> will not be disqualified. (1 Corinthians 9:26–27
> NASB)

Set

All athletes need to go through this, but most would rather skip it if it were possible. It's probably the part of sports that is the least fun. Yet this is also the part that separates average athletes from top athletes. Have you figured it out yet? It's training. Athletic training involves many different things: a proper diet, weight training, and practice are all necessary to get into top playing condition.

As Christians, we need to be training ourselves spiritually. This involves getting sin out of our lives and removing those things that may not be sin but are hindrances in our respective walks with Christ.

An example of this is when the love for sports begin to erode your devotion and fellowship time with God. Paul tells us in 1 Corinthians 9:27 that he trains spiritually so that he does not become disqualified for the prize. If a person comes into a game when he hasn't been practicing or is out of shape, he is not qualified to play. He will put up an abysmal performance.

The same is true in our spiritual lives. We need to continually bring ourselves under God's command so that we remain qualified for what He has called us to do. Just like Paul, we have to press on toward the prize.

Go

Are there sins in your life that you realize you need to remove?

1. Are there hindrances in your spiritual life that you need to get rid of?
2. Are you continually keeping yourself under God's command so that you can stay focused on the prize?

Workout

Hebrews 12:1–3

Overtime

God, I want to win the prize. Help me to strictly keep all eternal principles. Please show me the areas in my life where I need to train harder. Open my heart to the teaching of the Holy Spirit. Amen.

7

FOUNDATIONAL PRINCIPLES

> God created man in His own image, in the
> image of God He created him; male and female
> He created them. (Gen. 1:27 NASB)

No longer are you to walk around with your head hung low, with no understanding of who you are and where you come from. No longer should you be lied to about your true identity. Today, the identity crisis is completely over.

God deemed it fit to create you in His image, and there has never been any species that has been held in such high regard than human beings in the eyes of the Creator. You and I were created with certain inherent moral, ethical, and intellectual abilities. We are living symbols of God Himself on earth to represent His reign. God made no mistakes in creating you.

For so long, you have been tricked to believe that you cannot shake off the immoral things you do. But now you know that you can, because you were created with godly morals and now you can live a righteous life with your new knowledge. Now you are capable of conducting yourself in a manner that glorifies God. You are God's representative of goodness that the world needs, and you have been equipped from birth with intellectual and physical abilities to exhibit this goodness.

As believers, unlike the world, our thinking should be renewed and different. To some degree the world's thinking pattern affects believers, yet our understanding must be premised on the Word of God, not human psychology. For example, Psalm 91 sharpens our knowledge about security, 1 Corinthians 13 teaches us to love, and Hebrews 11 educates us on faith.

> He who dwells in the shelter of the Most High will abide in the shadow of the Almighty. I will say to the Lord, My refuge and my fortress, My God, in whom I trust! (Psalm 91:1–2 NASB)

In the first line, the psalmist writes about the secret place. Where is the secret place where we live under the shelter of God? Jesus said:

> But you, when you pray, go into your inner room, close your door and pray to your Father who is in secret, and your father who sees what is done in secret will reward you. (Matthew 6:6 NASB)

In the second verse, the psalmist says the Lord is our refuge and fortress and we should trust in Him. This confession is from a person who lives a secure life. If you go into your secret place and feel insecure about your finances, looks, or relationships, then where will you turn? Where you turn will be your security. You should turn to God. I will not put my trust and security in relationships, money, or people.

"God, You are the only One who can give me real security."

I am going to say that with my mouth—it is my confession. It comes from my personal relationship with God. The psalmist continues with some marvelous promises:

> For it is He who delivers you from the snare of the trapper and from the deadly pestilence. He will cover you with His pinions, and under His wings you may seek refuge; His faithfulness is a shield and bulwark. You will not be afraid of the terror by night, or of the arrow that flies by day; of the pestilence that stalks in darkness, or of the destruction that lays waste at noon. A thousand may fall at your side and ten thousand at your right hand, but it shall not approach you. You will only look on with your eyes and see the recompense of the wicked. For you have made the Lord, my refuge, even the Most High, your dwelling place. No evil will befall you, nor will any plague come near your tent. For He will give His angels charge concerning you, to guard you in all your ways. They will bear you up in their hands, that you do not strike your foot against a stone. You will tread upon the lion and cobra, the young lion and the serpent you will trample down. (Psalm 91:3–13 NASB)

This confession comes from an individual who is confident and secured in God. With these promises, you must not live your life in fear and insecurity. You should be a confident warrior regardless of the number of your enemies.

Thank God, this incredible promise from the Lord starts and ends with Him—God.

> Because he has loved Me, therefore I will deliver
> him; I will set him securely on high, because he
> has known My name. He will call upon Me, and
> I will answer him; I will be with him in trouble;
> I will rescue him and honor him. With long life
> I will satisfy him and let him see My salvation.
> (Psalm 91:14–16 NASB)

"I will show him My salvation." Isn't this an awesome promise? This is God's promise to you, if you will turn to Him in prayer and believe in Him. These are your foundational principles.

You are who you are and no one can superimpose their own ideas and beliefs on the truth that has now been revealed to you. No longer shall you live in the shadow of another, or the shadow of fear that has eclipsed your true persona that the world so desperately desires. You have been created with great reverence, heartfelt interest, and respect. There were no mistakes when God created you, for this is the foundation that can never fail. You are God's unique and set-apart being who has been placed in this world for a specific assignment and a specific time. In wonderment, a conversation ensued in heaven that unveils how unique you are.

> What is man that You take thought of him, and
> the son of man that You care for him? (Psalm
> 8:4 NASB)

When you become aware of your God-given uniqueness, what bothers you will bother you no more. Then, it becomes easy to turn every anxious and worrisome thought into prayer until you have victory. Remember Paul's words to the Philippians:

> Be anxious for nothing, but in everything by prayer and supplication with thanksgiving let your requests be made known to God. And the peace of God, which surpasses all comprehension, will guard your hearts and your minds in Christ Jesus. (Philippians 4:6–7 NASB)

Every morning when you wake up, in addition to your prayer list, have a worry list—a list that says, *this is what is bothering me today.* Many times, when you are trying to pray, your mind may wander. Do you know where it usually travels? To those things that bother you. You may have a meeting today with a boss you don't like. Perhaps you have a test to take this afternoon. You might have a money problem. So make your worry list a part of your new prayer list.

Paul wanted the Philippians to make their requests known to God with thanksgiving. That means that we should thank Him that He loves, hears, and will answer our prayers. Say, "Thank you, Father, because You love me, You care for me, You know everything that is happening in my life, and You will hear and answer me." The devil wants you to think that you are on your own and that you have to solve your own problems.

He is a liar! You have a loving Father who wants to help you in every circumstance. If you are sitting around worrying, you are wasting that relationship. Nothing could give you more comfort. If Bill Gates were your father, you would probably think that you would never have to worry about anything ever again, because of the access to all the money in the world, right? Well, your Heavenly Father is the creator of Bill Gates, and has no need for money as He owns everything here on earth and in the cosmos.

When you have prayed through your worry and anxiety,

the Bible says you will have peace. The saints of old come to mind; they know how to "pray through" an issue. They would pray until they got peace, which will guard their mind and heart. The Greek word for "guard" is *phroureō*, which means to guard against a military invasion.

Thank God for everything. He will set a military guard around your heart so that the devil cannot penetrate it with worry and anxiety. Be practical about your prayer life. What is coming against you? Grab hold of your Fathers hand and attack it. Kill the adversaries of your life first thing in the morning so that you can have a seamless and testimony-filled day. Ruin them before they dare ruin your life. Walk with God.

HAVE FAITH AND CONFESS GOD'S LOVE

Believe and confess that God is your loving Father and that He cares for you. Remember what Jesus said:

> Do not worry then, saying, what will we eat? Or what will we drink? Or what will we wear for clothing? For the gentiles eagerly seek all these things; for your heavenly Father knows that you need all these things. But seek first His kingdom and His righteousness, and all these things will be added to you. (Matthew 6:31–33 NASB)

You have the best Father in the world, and He is your answer to every worry and anxiety. Hence, rest upon Him, for He cares for you. Bid farewell to anxiety and worry and welcome His rest and peace that supersede human comprehension.

REFLECT ON YOUR FOUNDATION ONCE MORE

Who are you?

Ready

> And He summoned the crowed with His
> disciples, and said to them, if anyone wishes to
> come after Me, he must deny himself, and take
> up his cross and follow Me. (Mark 8:34 NASB)

Set

Some of the most common questions posed to sports fans are, "Who do you follow? I'm a Denver fan." "I follow the University of North Carolina." "I'm a Hoosier." No matter how you phrase it, we all follow one team or another. This applies to our lives in Christ as well. It is not uncommon today to hear believers ask, "What denomination are you?" Some say, "I am a Baptist." Others claim to be Methodist, Lutheran, Catholic, and so on. This has always disturbed me in no small way.

I am so proud of my Christian upbringing and the denominational truths that I have learned over the years, but when I accepted Jesus Christ as Lord and Savior of my life, I committed to Him. I didn't commit to some set of religious traditions or legalistic dos and don'ts. The Team FCA Competitor's Creed states: "I am a Christian first and last. ..." So when people ask me today what I am spiritually, I simply tell them that I am a Christian who happens to attend a Biblical church. Jesus Christ, who is our perfect example, is whom we must follow and imitate. I am His.

Please do not misunderstand me. I am not bashing your denominational preference. But do understand that the denomination in which you have been raised is nothing without the relationship you can have—and need to have—with Jesus Christ. If you want to get caught up in anything, get caught up in the doctrine of Jesus Christ and His Word. To find out more, go to your Bible and begin to read more about Him.

Jere Johnson once answerd a question he was asked this way; What are you? As for me and my household, we tell others, "I am a Christian first and last!" I hope you can say that, too!

Go

1. Whom or what do you follow?
2. Are you caught up in the dos and don'ts of your faith, or are you caught up in Jesus Christ?
3. Do you know how to begin the journey to becoming who you are in Christ Jesus? (If not, read the four gospels— Matthew, Mark, Luke, and John, or find someone who can point you in the right direction!)

Workout

Joshua 24:15; Psalms 111:9–11; John 14:6

Overtime

Father, thank You for Your Son. Help me to rest and find my sole foundation in Him.

CONCLUSION

You must have heard the maxim, "it's not about what is being asked of you, but rather if you would do it which makes a huge difference in the end." One of Jesus's parables provides a powerful example of this simple truth:

> But what do you think? A man had two sons, and he came to the first and said, Son, go work today in the vineyard. And he answered, I will not; but afterward he regretted it and went. The man came to the second and said the same thing; and he answered, I will, sir; but he did not go. Which of the two did the will of his father? They said, the first. Jesus said to them, truly I say to you that the tax collectors and prostitutes will get into the kingdom of God before you. For John came to you in the way of righteousness and you did not believe him; But the tax collectors and prostitutes did believe him; and you, seeing this, did not even feel remorse afterward so as to believe him. (Matthew 21:28–32 NASB)

Change is a constant in life, and it has been clearly revealed in this book that we have a choice of how and what we change.

As Paul said in the book of Romans, we are changed—transformed—by the renewal of our minds. God wants to transform our minds, not only so we think differently but also as a means of transforming our behavior, for we are created to do good works (Ephesians 2:10). When our minds have been renewed and retrofitted in Christ, we will understand God's perfect will for our lives and move toward spiritual maturity.

Coming into full spiritual maturity enables us to pursue our highest spiritual and physical goals.

I press on toward the goal for the prize of the upward call of God in Christ Jesus. (Philippians 3:14 NASB).

Our kingdom race is a marathon, not a sprint. Some key principles that are required for the successful completion of your kingdom race have been shared with you in this book. Just like the sons of the man in Matthew 21, you have a choice to make when it comes to the matter of change. Now is the time for you to be made new with the necessary components that your life did not have years ago to possess today all that the Lord has designed you to be. May the good Lord help you to be Retrofit. Amen.

Printed in the United States
by Baker & Taylor Publisher Services